The Australia...

Guide to the Snakes of South-East Australia

AUSTRALIAN REPTILE PARK
PO Box 192, Gosford, NSW
Telephone (043) 28 4311
First Published 1990 by
Weigel Photoscript

Reprinted 2007

Designed and Written by John Weigel

Typesetting by Jill Rassack,
Silicon Quill, Hornsby Heights, NSW
Printed in Singapore
ISBN 0-646-00006-3

To My Parents

Contents

Preface

Snakes of South-East Australia is my third self-publishing venture. It follows *Care of Australian Reptiles in Captivity* (1988, now in its third printing) and *The Australian Reptile Park Story* (1989, now in its second printing). This book, like the others, would not have happened without a great deal of endurance and patience from Robyn. Glenn Shea had significant input into the book's form and format, and provided much-needed technical information regarding the snakes. I am more than ever indebted to Glenn for his help and friendship. Dr Richard Shine also read the manuscript and provided helpful comments; his consistent support and encouragement over the years is warmly appreciated. Mark Hutchinson and Margaret Charles also commented on drafts.

Information on the distributions, colour varations and ecology of the snakes is drawn heavily from the publications of Dr Harold Cogger (various books on the reptiles of Australia, especially *Reptiles and Amphibians of Australia* (1986) Reed, Australia); Dr Richard Shine (the very numerous scientific papers on snake ecology that he has published during the past 20 years); and Steve Wilson and David Knowles (their book *Australia's Reptiles* (1988) Collins, Australia).

I am greatly indebted to the photographers, who added so much to the nature of this publication. Mark Hutchinson kindly provided a broad selection of his excellent photographs, as did Peter Robertson, Steve Wilson, Glenn Shea and Greg Parker. Additional photographs of equal standard were kindly provided by Robert Cook, Dr Harold Cogger, Gary Stephenson, Alex Dudley and Grant Husband. Photographs are individually credited or are the work of the author.

Sharon Postlethwaite produced all of the excellent line drawings of the snakes used in the identification keys, as well as the marvellous paintings that appear on the front cover.

Dr Struan Sutherland of the Commonwealth Serum Laboratories kindly permitted use of the schematic diagrams depicting the pressure/immobilization first aid treatment for snake-bite that he and his research team first introduced in 1979. The Australian Reptile Park has enjoyed a long association with Dr Sutherland, providing spider and snake venoms during his ground-breaking research into the treatment of bites and stings of venomous creatures.

Patience and hard work from Jill Rassack of Silicon Quill and Yuri Claussen of Dai Nippon are greatly appreciated. The high quality of Dai Nippon printing speaks for itself.

Finally, I wish to thank the keepers and office staff at the Reptile Park for allowing me the time needed to complete the project, and especially Lyn Abra for secretarial assistance above and beyond the call of duty, Alex Innes and Irwynne Symington for encouragement and Ted Osbaldeston for first suggesting the need for such a publication.

Introduction

Learning to identify the snakes you encounter, either while bushwalking or in your own backyard, can be fun and challenging. Also, an increasing familiarity with the appearance and habits of the dangerous species will reduce your likelihood of being bitten. This publication is intended for easy use by the non-expert, without complex technical information. If greater detail is needed, it can be found in other, more comprehensive volumes. This book has been produced in recognition of the fact that many people are interested, if not a little worried about the snakes they are most likely to encounter, but are unlikely to purchase an expensive, and necessarily cumbersome edition when only a small portion of its contents are devoted to their local snake fauna.

Guide to the Snakes of South-East Australia is intended to be used as a field guide; it is designed to travel in the pocket or day pack and fully covers the 50 species of terrestrial snakes occuring in the south-eastern corner of Australia - an area defined by the shaded portion of the map on the front cover. Although this area includes more than 80% of the nation's inhabitants and contains their favorite recreation spots, it is shared by only about a third of Australia's snake species. In concentrating on these species alone, the task of accurate snake identification becomes much easier for the reader.

The species identification section includes 137 colour photographs. The range maps are intended to make identification simpler. In some cases, where two similar species have discretely separate geographical distributions as portrayed by the maps, little effort has been made to define further distinguishing characteristics.

Where two species are similar in colour patterns as well as body shapes and geographic distributions, the only reliable means of identifying a snake is to examine the body scales or possibly some other physical details. Therefore a snake identification 'key', based largely upon differing scale conditions amongst the species is presented for positive identification of specimens. All snake measurements refer to the total length from snout to tip of tail.

It is not the author's intention to encourage the catching and handling of potentially dangerous snakes, nor the killing of specimens to facilitate identification. Rather, the key is intended for identification of specimens that are found dead, or for those that are clearly members of non-venomous families. For example, snakes of the family Typhlopidae, although easily recognized as harmless 'worm snakes' upon gross inspection, are practically impossible to further distinguish between the various species without considering scale conditions.

When using the identification section, remember that the identification keys, photographs, range maps, descriptions, habits, etc only refer to specimens originating from within the defined South-East.

Introductory and background information on the various families of snakes of the South-East is provided. A supplemental section further deals with the dangerously venomous species; how to avoid them, what to do if they are encountered, and the recommended first aid treatment for snake-bite.

The matter of captive maintenance of snakes is discussed, but specific advice on reptile husbandry has not been included. This subject is complex, and best not dealt with superficially (as it traditionally has been in reptile identification books), leaving the hobbyist with just enough information to get himself (or more to the point, his charges) into trouble. My earlier work *Care of Australian Reptiles in Captivity* deals with this subject adequately. It is distributed by Gordon and Gotch and available upon request or order from most Australian bookshops.

General Characteristics of Snakes

REPTILES

The reptiles were the first vertebrate group to truly colonize the land. They first appeared about 300 million years ago and dominated the earth until the end of the age of dinosaurs some 65 million years ago. Today there are about 6,000 reptile species in the world, making them more numerous than mammals. Living reptiles can be divided into six groups: the tortoises and turtles; the crocodiles and alligators; the 'beak-heads', with just one species - the New Zealand tuatara; the amphisbaenians or worm lizards (a small group of worm-like burrowers that do not occur in Australia); the lizards and the snakes. Lizards (over 3,500 species worldwide) and snakes (almost 2,500 species worldwide) share a common ancestry and are both included in the order Squamata. There is little fossil evidence suggesting exactly how and when the snakes first appeared. The oldest known snake fossil dates back to around 130 million years ago.

Modern reptile species are not degenerate or inferior in comparison to birds and mammals; they simply go about things in different ways and are in many respects just as successful. They are commonly considered inferior on account of being "cold-blooded" in contrast to the "warm-blooded" birds and mammals. These terms are now thought misleading and are rarely used by biologists. Most mammals and birds maintain very steady, warm body temperatures by metabolizing large amounts of food. Reptiles on the other hand rely mainly upon the sun, directly or indirectly, to raise their body temperature when activity is required. By shuttling between locations of higher and lower temperature, reptiles can maintain a similar body temperature to mammals while requiring only a tenth as much food. When body heat is not required for activity they can rest in a position where their temperature remains much lower and save the energy that mammals and birds waste in such conditions. In areas where winter temperatures are too low to allow reptile activity, they may shelter in a cool underground hideaway until springtime warming stimulates renewed activity.

SNAKES

Snakes can be distinguished from most of the other reptiles by their elongate, limbless form combined with having a long forked tongue and lacking eyelids and ear openings. Being long and thin allows snakes to move through narrow gaps and into burrows in the pursuit of prey. Trees can be easily climbed by most, and limbless movement allows stealth when hunting. An additional advantage to limblessness is the ability to warm and cool the body very quickly when moving in and out of the sun or warm positions due to the large amount of surface area in relation to body mass. Following exposure to warmth, snakes are able to retain body warmth by coiling tightly to reduce the amount of body surface exposed to cooler surroundings.

The distinction between snakes and some lizards can be subtle. Several south-eastern lizard species (all less than 70 cm long) have elongated bodies and are legless or nearly legless, with only tiny rudimentary limbs or flap-like vestiges that are usually held flat against the base of the tail and hence may not be obvious. These species differ from snakes in having flat, not forked tongues, in lacking the broad transverse belly scales of snakes, and in the majority of cases, by having visible ear openings.

No snakes are slimy. Although there are snakes adapted to life in the water, the skin of these will dry to reveal scaly skin. All snakes periodically slough their outer layer of skin. The frequency of sloughs depends upon the rate of growth and levels of activity. Lustre and colour increase after sloughing is complete and the beautiful colours and patterns of some species can be quite impressive.

All snakes are predators with prey ranging from the ants and termites eaten by tiny worm snakes, to the small mammals and birds eaten by many of the larger species. Frogs and lizards are the staple diet of many south-eastern snake species. Constriction is employed by some species for overpowering and killing their prey, while others use toxic venoms. Some use neither, and simply swallow their struggling prey.

Snakes do not normally feed on a daily basis, but are opportunistic hunters, gorging themselves when food is plentiful, while at other times fasting for weeks or even months at a time. The snakes at the Australian Reptile Park are fed once every week or fortnight, often resulting in a faster rate of growth than that of wild specimens. Whatever is eaten must be eaten whole and is usually eaten head first for ease of swallowing. Since the two sides of the lower jaw do not connect to form a chin, snakes can spread the elastic skin and tissue between to accommodate suprisingly large meals. Such a meal may take a week or more to be digested and eliminated.

Although some snakes, including Whip Snakes, Tree snakes and Brown snakes have fairly keen eye-sight, most do not. None have external ears and it is believed that they have only a poor sense of hearing. Instead, most snakes rely heavily upon a keen sense of smell in the location of food, the avoidance of predators and in generally perceiving their environments. With their lower metabolic rate, snakes take fewer breaths than birds or mammals, and 'sniffing' is therefore not an effective means of smelling. Instead, they use their long forked tongues to 'taste' the ground and air in order to detect scents. The tongue is waved intermittently, thus collecting scent particles that are brought into the mouth and introduced to the Jacobson's organ, a reptilian organ of smell, positioned in the roof of the mouth. To track their prey, snakes follow scent trails left behind by their prey, often ambushing their victims within burrows and other retreats.

An additional means of prey detection is used by the pythons. Pits along the upper and/or lower lips contain tiny heat-detecting organs, useful in the location of warm-blooded prey on even the darkest of nights.

Most snakes have seasonal breeding habits. Mating usually occurs in spring or autumn, depending upon the species. Egg-laying species deposit soft, leathery eggs, usually in early summer, hatching between 40 and 70 days later. These are typically deposited in burrows or beneath stones or fallen timber. Other species produce live young, usually in the summer. Whether it is a clutch of eggs or a brood of live young that is produced, most species show no maternal care. Young snakes must fend for themselves from the day they are born or hatched, and only the pythons protect their eggs until hatching commences.

HOW SNAKES ARE CLASSIFIED

To help understand how and why the snakes of the South-East are assigned to various species and families, it is important to know how scientists classify snakes. Each kind of animal is given a unique combination of two names - a genus name and a species name. These do the same job as our christian names and surnames, only the other way around. With animal names the genus names always comes first, and works just like our surname by linking together species that are closely related. For example, the Swamp Snake, as it is known in some areas, is also known as the Marsh Snake in others, leading to a certain amount of confusion. However, it is always known by scientists as *Hemiaspis signata*. It is closely related to the Grey Snake *Hemiaspis damelii*, but less closely related to the White-lipped Snake *Drysdalia coronoides*, as is reflected in its different genus name.

Each kind of snake is assigned to a species, and similar species are grouped into a genus. Similar genera (plural of genus) are then grouped into a family. The Swamp Snake, Grey Snake and White-lipped Snake are all included in the same family - Elapidae. The elapids are front-fanged terrestrial venomous snakes.

Four families of terrestrial snakes occur in the South-East. Most species belong to the venomous Elapidae. Other families include the pythons (family Boidae), the worm snakes (family Typhlopidae) and the colubrid snakes - (family Colubridae).

Snakes of South-East Australia

WORM SNAKES (Family Typhlopidae)

The greatest number of Australia's non-venomous snakes are of the widespread family Typhlopidae. Seven of these tiny burrowing snakes occur in the South-East where they are known familiarly as 'worm snakes' due to their earthworm-like appearance, or 'blind snakes' because of their greatly reduced eyes. All are included in the genus *Ramphotyphlops* and are so similar that accurate field identification can be very difficult.

Worm snakes are armoured with smooth overlapping scales extending from tail to snout. The body is cylindrical and terminates at either end rather abruptly. The tail is very short and stumpy, ending with a small conical spine. The head is as unobtrusive as the tail, with greatly reduced eyes that appear as no more than tiny pigmented spots, and are covered by thick semi-transparent scales.

Most of the worm snake's life is spent underground. Whether it creates its own burrows, or relies upon ant and termite tunnels is not known. Its diet consists almost exclusively of ants and termites and especially their eggs, larvae and pupae. Once inside a termite or ant colony, a worm snake may gorge itself freely upon the inhabitants which bite without effect at the snake's scaly armour. The manner in which the worm snake swallows its meal is unusual amongst snakes; by some unexplained mechanism it appears to 'suck' its food items down with minimal movement of the jaws.

Its tail spine has a separate function in assisting movement through narrow tunnels and burrows; it is planted against the sides of these to provide 'footing' from which the body can be pushed forwards before being gathered again for another push forward.

A worm snake's rudimentary eyes could have only limited use underground, and its not known how much use they are when the snake does occasionally surface. Movement above ground occurs only at night and is most frequent following heavy rains which presumably flood underground burrows and tunnels.

If molested, it is not likely (if in fact it is able) to bite, but is not without defence; a foul-smelling fluid is excreted, and it may poke at its antagonist with its spinous tail-tip. When used against human beings the spine does not even penetrate the skin, but it does create a spontaneous reaction of surprise – usually resulting in the snake being dropped or thrown.

PYTHONS (Family Boidae)

Pythons are thought to be amongst the most primitive of the world's snakes; fossilized python bones have turned up in various parts of the world dating back more than 70 million years. One early Australian species *Montypythonoides riversleighensis* grew to seven metres. The longest modern Australian species is the Scrub Python *Morelia amethystina* of north Queensland, for which there are reports of specimens as long as six metres. Pythons are unusual in that they breathe with 2 lungs; other snake families have reduced that number to one. Pythons also possess vestiges of hind limbs. These tiny "spurs", positioned one on either side of the vent, are used by males to tickle and entice females prior to mating.

Pythons are the only snakes known to truly incubate their eggs. Clutch temperatures may be maintained above air temperature as the protective female python coils around her eggs. She will shiver and twitch, behaviours which generate heat to warm the eggs. While coiled around the eggs for the 40 to 70 days of incubation, the mother is able to protect the clutch from predation. She will not eat during this time.

Most pythons have a series of heat-sensing pits positioned along the lower and/or upper lips. In effect, this sensory system provides an alternative vision - as seen through the usually invisible infra-red spectrum of light. Since each object radiates a slightly different amount of heat than other objects around it, the python can detect its prey during even the darkest of nights.

The Eastern Children's Python *Liasis maculosus* inhabits rocky outcrops in the northern part of the South-East region. It is rarely encountered because of its secretive nature and patchy distribution within the region, but it is widespread and commonly encountered further north along the Queensland coast.

The Diamond Python *Morelia spilota spilota* and the Carpet Python *Morelia spilota variegata* differ from one another primarily in colouration. Both are well known for their habit of entering rural buildings and homes where they rest by day amongst rafters or below floor boards. Some people condemn intruding pythons as a threat to chickens or household pets, while others recognize their value as a natural control over rats and mice. Although primarily nocturnal, during the wintertime Diamond Pythons and Carpet Pythons may be observed sun basking in tree tops or rock crevices.

COLUBRID SNAKES (Family Colubridae)

Nearly two-thirds of the world's snake species belong to the family Colubridae. In most countries, the colubrid snakes are popularly referred to as the 'typical' snakes. This is not so in Australia however, where only ten species occur, three of which enter the South-East.

The Freshwater Snake or 'Keelback' *Tropidonophis mairii* usually lives along the banks of freshwater streams or in swampy country where it feeds mainly upon frogs, which it hunts at night.

The Brown Tree Snake *Boiga irregularis* and the Green Tree Snake *Dendrelaphis punctulatus* are both well suited to climbing – not only in trees but amongst rocky outcrops, where they can withdraw into deep, protective crevices. In order to span the distances between branches or rocks, tree snakes have especially elongated bodies. Their long, slender tails provide support when wrapped around the branches of trees or the irregularities of rock surfaces. Both species are commonly found inhabiting hollow walls and ceiling recesses in rural homes. The Green Tree Snake is active mainly by day, feeding principally upon frogs. The Brown Tree Snake is more likely to inhabit deep sandstone crevices than tree hollows, and emerges at night to forage for lizards, small mammals and birds. It has a primitive venom apparatus and a mildly toxic venom that is not regarded as dangerous to human beings. Its tiny grooved venom-conducting fangs are positioned well to the back of the upper jaw, meaning that it must partially swallow its prey in order to work the fangs into it.

ELAPID SNAKES (Family Elapidae)

The largest proportion of Australia's species of snakes belong to the family Elapidae, characterised by having venom-conducting fangs positioned towards the front of the upper jaw. The fangs of the various elapid species vary in lengths. In the smallest species they would be barely adequate to pierce human skin, while the fangs of the largest species can exceed 10 mm in length. The fangs are regularly replaced by new ones as they tend to be broken or lost in the normal wear and tear of biting.

Snake venoms are comprised of proteins and protein-like molecules. Each elapid snake species has its own unique venom which may serve several purposes. Venoms are used to kill prey and may have specific qualities that severely affect their preferred prey type while having only a lesser affect upon other types of animals. Some snake venom components act as enzymes to speed the digestion of food, breaking down tissue within the prey animal which would otherwise be digested only from the outer surface inward. Many elapids also use their toxic venoms as a defence against predators.

The elapid species most likely to be encountered around the home and garden are mainly small, shy and innocuous. They are usually turned up during gardening and clearing activities. These include the 'Dwarf' Snakes – genus *Cacophis*, Crowned Snakes – genus *Drysdalia*, Hooded Snakes – genus *Unechis*, and the Swamp Snake *Hemiaspis signata*. All of these snakes are very similar in size (to about 40 cm), body form and colour pattern. All feed mainly on frogs or skinks. Crowned Snakes and Swamp Snakes are diurnal; Dwarf and Hooded Snakes are nocturnal.

Numerous small elapid species also inhabit arid inland districts as well. The Curl Snake *Denisonia suta* is common in the most desolate and barren of inland and arid regions. If tormented, the Curl Snake forms loops with its body – hence its common name, from which it may flail about wildly in an attempt to bite. Like most of the small elapids, its bite would be likely to cause considerable discomfort, but would not be regarded as potentially lethal. Other small inland species include the De Vis' banded snake *Denisonia devisii* and the Bardick *Echiopsis curta*.

There are several species of burrowing elapids inhabiting the south-east. These occasionally emerge at night but spend most of the time submerged in loose sand or within burrows in harder packed soils. The Bandy Bandy *Vermicella annulata* is a beautifully marked species with broad rings of black and white alternately encircling the body. It preys almost exclusively upon worm snakes (genus *Ramphotyphlops*). If threatened, the Bandy-bandy arches one or two loops of its body high above the ground and may hold this position for some time, but is not likely to bite, even when handled. The nature of its venom is unknown.

Two other attractive burrowing species are the Desert Burrowing Snake *Simoselaps bertholdi* - a very colourful species with alternating orange and black rings around the body, and the Coral Snake *S. australis* which is predominantly red with narrow cream bands. Both species prey upon small skinks, but the Coral Snake is unusual in that it is also known to eat the eggs of snakes and lizards. Special teeth situated at the back of the upper jaw slice the leathery eggs as they are swallowed, allowing digestion of the nutritious contents.

Eastern forests are inhabited by three nocturnal, semi-arboreal elapid snakes included in the genus *Hoplocephalus*. These are medium-sized snakes (from 0.5 m to 0.8 m) and are regarded as potentially dangerous. Symptoms from their bites vary, but may include intense pain and local swelling coupled with severe headache, nausea and disorientation. The Broad-headed Snake *Hoplocephalus bungaroides* lives amongst sandstone outcrops where it shelters beneath flat exfoliations of the sandstone. The use of 'bush-rock' in Sydney gardens has seen the loss of suitable habitat for this species and as a result it is now considered to be an endangered species.

The Whip snakes (genus *Demansia*) are slender, fast moving, agile species that range widely by day in search of prey. The Yellow-faced Whip Snake *D. psammophis* is commonly encountered throughout most of the South-East, though it barely reaches Victoria and south-eastern South Australia. The Black Whip Snake *D. atra* occurs only in the northern reaches of the South-East. Both species grow to about a metre.

The Death Adder *Acanthophis antarcticus* is proportionately the most robust of Australian snake species. Its head is very broad and distinct from its neck, and its body is quite thick. The Death Adder is an ambush feeder with an unusual hunting strategy. It partially buries itself amongst fallen leaf litter, its well camouflaged by broken colour pattern (usually of lighter and darker bands of red, brown or grey), to await the approach of its prey. The tip of its tail, which is modified to resemble a small caterpillar, is wriggled insect-like before its snout in an attempt to lure the attention of any hungry lizard, small mammal or bird that might be inticed into striking range. Defensively, the Death Adder flattens itself out and may strike savagely. Fortunately, victims of bites from this dangerously venomous species generally respond well to antivenom treatment.

The Red-bellied Black Snake *Pseudechis porphyriacus* is widespread throughout all but the driest environments in the South-East. Like many of the larger elapid species, males grow considerably larger than females; males commonly exceeding one and a half metres, while females attain a length of only about a metre. The Spotted Black Snake *Pseudechis guttatus* is found from mid-eastern New South Wales to south-eastern Queensland, while the King Brown Snake *Pseudechis australis* (not to be confused with the true Brown snakes (genus *Pseudonaja*) is found only in arid inland districts. Both are large, dangerously venomous species.

Three species of Brown snakes (genus *Pseudonaja*) enter the South-East. One of these, the Five-ringed Snake *P. modesta*, grows to only 0.6 m and is a shy, nocturnal species, but the other two are large and fast moving. The Eastern Brown Snake *P. textilis* and the Western Brown Snake *P. nuchalis* are both highly venomous, easily agitated species. The Eastern Brown is quite common throughout most of the region. It ranges widely by day in search of mice, often entering inhabited areas in search of its prey. If cornered, the body is raised high in 'S' shaped loops, and strikes may be directed forward as far as half the length of the body. The Western Brown ranges throughout arid and semi-arid inland districts, where its distribution partly overlaps with that of the Eastern Brown.

The Taipan *Oxyuranus scutellatus* is one of the biggest and most feared of all Australian snakes owing to its large size (to over two metres), extremely toxic venom, and nervous disposition. The Taipan does not hesitate to bite when cornered or attacked, and may inflict a series of savage bites in rapid succession. Nevertheless, much of the hysteria surrounding this species is unfounded, as it is not often encountered, being quite shy and very anxious to move away from approaching human beings. A northern species, it only just reaches the South-East region in the coast and hinterland of southern Queensland and just across the border into New South Wales, where it is very rare at this extremity of its distribution. Many of the unconfirmed sightings of this species are probably attributable to misidentified Eastern Brown Snakes.

The Tiger Snake *Notechis scutatus* is an inhabitant of cool moist habitats associated with most of the coastal fresh waterways of the South-East. It can also be found along river banks in some inland areas. Its attractive yellowish and brown bands are reflected in its given name, although unbanded specimens are common as well. The Black Tiger Snake *Notechis ater* is mainly an inhabitant of off-shore islands, including

Tasmania, but also occurs in two localized populations on mainland South Australia. Both Tiger snake species are sun-loving and spend a great deal of time basking, especially on sunny days when temperatures are cool, or during slightly overcast warm days. They feed mainly on frogs, and may be found in large numbers in well-watered regions with high frog populations. The venoms of these two species are very toxic and the Common Tiger Snake accounts for the majority of snake-bite deaths in Australia.

The Copperhead *Austrelaps superbus* is quite variable in colouration, with three different forms commonly recognized; a highlands form from moist alpine and subalpine habitats, a lowlands form from well watered environments at lower altitudes, and a pygmy form that attains a maximum length of only about a half a metre restricted to the Mt. Lofty Range of South Australia and nearby Kangaroo Island.

Copperheads are especially inoffensive snakes and disinclined to bite unless trodden on or handled. Their tolerance to cold weather is notable, and they may be active during early spring and late autumn when temperatures are too cold for most other reptile species. This species preys mainly on frogs.

The Rough-scaled Snake *Tropidechis carinatus* is usually found close to water in moist, forested country from mid-eastern New South Wales northwards – often at high altitude. It is active more often at night than by day, especially in warm weather, when frogs, small mammals, and lizards are hunted. This dangerously venomous species is frequently confused with the harmless Keelback, which is sometimes found in the same habitats and has similarly rugose body scales. Some scientists believe that the Rough-scaled Snake is a close relative to the Tiger Snake, perhaps correctly belonging within the same genus.

Identification Key for the Snakes of the South-East

The following identification key for snakes of the South-East consists of a series of numbered 'couplets' which give two contrasting statements. Choose the statement in the first couplet which best fits the snake to be identified and go on to the next couplet indicated. Repeat this process until one of the stements leads first to the relevant Family key, then to the name of the species, then check the specimen against the description and identification photographs for that species on the page indicated.

1 Skin slimy and/or without scales covering skin; body possibly of varying length .... **not a snake**
Body covered with overlapping scales which may be dull to highly glossy, but skin is *never* slimy **2**

2

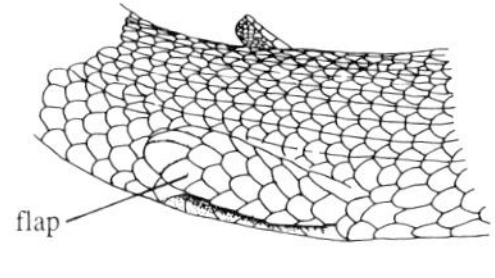

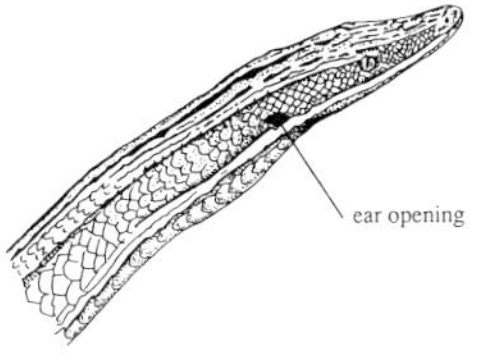

Figure adapted from *Australian Lizards and Snakes*, (1985) Collins.

Any of the following characteristics present: earholes; moveable eyelids; broad, unforked tongue; or visible appendages of any description, including paired scaly 'flaps' held flat against body on either side of anal region .... **a lizard, not a snake** (for photographs of some commonly encountered snake-like lizards, see pp 17-19)

None of the abovementioned characteristics present, unless a single pair of small spur-like claws exist, positioned with one on either side of the anal region *and* a row of heat-sensing pits are present in lower and possibly upper lips (see figure below).... **3**

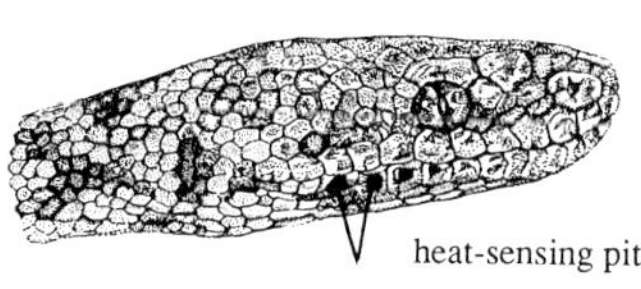

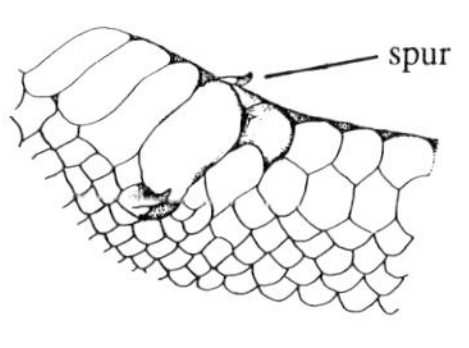

3 Tail is laterally compressed (flattened from side to side) and paddle-shaped, being as tall or nearly as tall as body; specimen found at sea's edge .... **sea snake** (dangerously venomous; sea snakes not discussed in this book)

Tail not compressed and paddle-shaped, but either tapering or with a rounded end bearing a small, thorn-like spine. .... **4 (terrestrial snake)**

sea snake tail

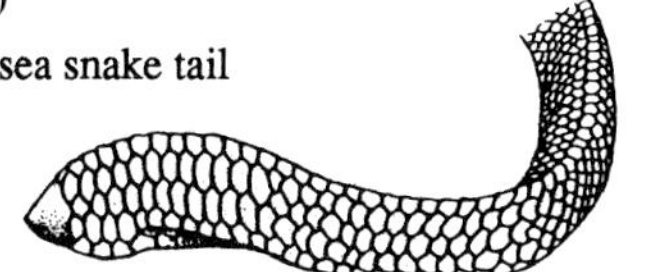

4 Row of pits along lower and possibly upper lips; a small spur present on either side of the vent .... **Family Boidae** (Pythons, not venomous) species identification key on page 26

No row of pits along lower or upper lips; no small spur near vent **5**

5 Tail very short, rounded and sausage-shaped, terminating in a tiny spur. Eyes represented by small dark spots covered over by thick scales; body scales evenly sized around body .... **Family Typhlopidae** (Worm Snakes, not venomous) species identification key on page 20

Tail is not rounded and sausage-shaped with tiny spur-like terminus; eyes well developed, not covered by a thick, opaque/ transluscent scale; belly scales substantially broader than other body scales **6**

6

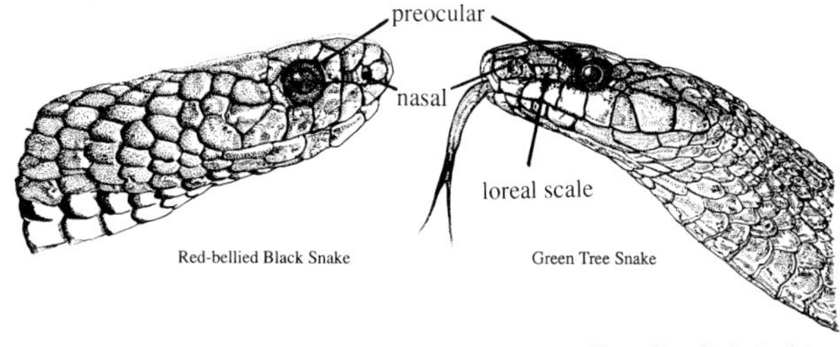

Red-bellied Black Snake Green Tree Snake

Loreal scale(s) present .... **Family Colubridae** (Colubrid Snakes, not dangerous) species identification key on page 30

No loreal scale(s) present............................... **Family Elapidae** (Front-fanged Venomous Snakes) species identification key on page 33

Numerous snake-like lizard species inhabit the South-East. Some representative species are pictured on pp 17-19. To distinguish between snakes and lizards refer to couplet 2 in Key to the Snakes of the South-East, page 15.

She-oak Skink *Cyclodomorphus casuarinae*

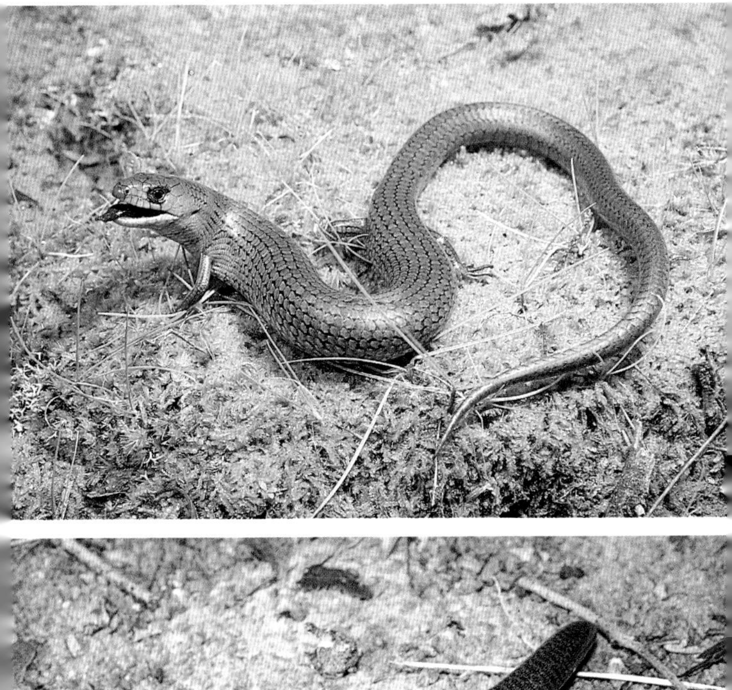

Alex Dudley

Leuckart's Skink *Anomalopus leuckartii*

Burton's Legless Lizard *Lialis burtonis*

Common Scaly-foot *Pygopus lepidopodus*

Hooded Scaly-foot *Pygopus nigriceps*

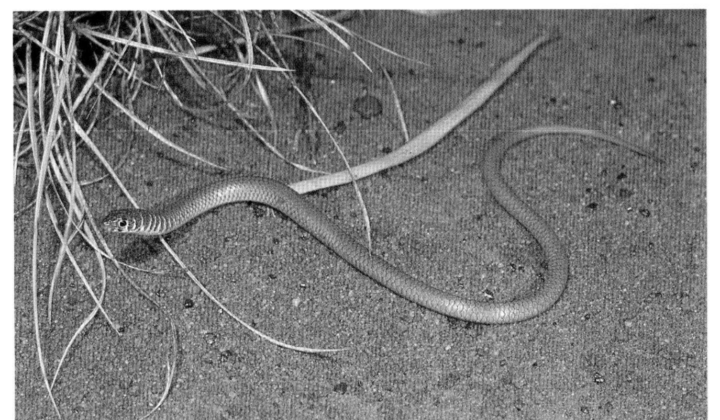

Legless Lizard *Delma australis*

Glenn Shea

Legless Lizard *Delma inornata*

Legless Lizard *Aprasia inaurita*

Key to the Family Typhlopidae (Worm Snakes)

All Worm Snake species are difficult to distinguish from one another without diagnosing relevant scale conditions. All are small, worm-like burrowing snakes belonging to the same genus (*Ramphotyphlops*). Seven species occur in the South-East; several additional species have been portrayed as entering the region, but these reports are based on dubious old records unconfirmed in modern collections.

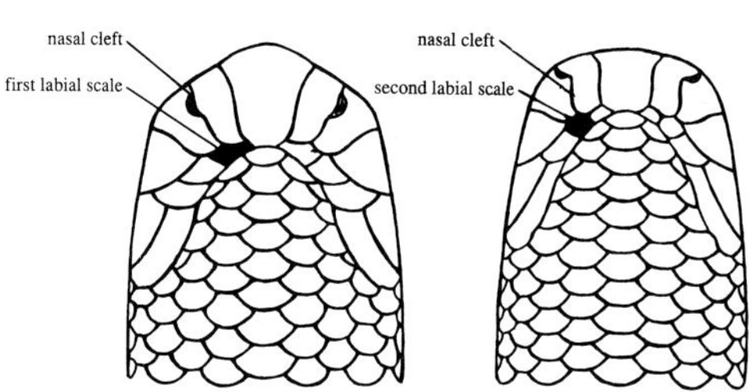

When counting the number of scale ro[w]
midbody, begin at the approximate mi[d]
of the snake's body. Begin with a body s[cale]
immediately above and adjacent to a b[elly]
scale (in Worm Snakes the belly scale[s]
not much bigger than body scales but ca[n]
distinguished by their central posit[ion].
Count diagonally until another belly sc[ale]
contacted. Do not include the belly scal[e]
the total midbody scale count.

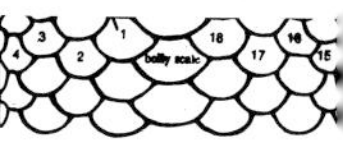

1 Nasal cleft contacting first labial scale **2**
Nasal cleft contacting second labial scale **3**

2 Body in 20 scale rows at mid-body .... ***R. proximus*** (page 25)
Body in 22 scale rows at mid-body ..... ***R. nigrescens*** (page 24)
Body in 24 scale rows at mid-body .... ***R. ligatus*** (page 23)

3 Body in 18 scale rows at mid-body .... ***R. affinis*** (page 21)
Body in 20 scale rows at mid-body **4**
Body in 22 scale rows at mid-body .... ***R. australis*** (page 22)

4 Snout trilobed .... ***R. bituberculatus*** (page 23)
Snout bluntly rounded .... ***R. wiedii*** (page 25)

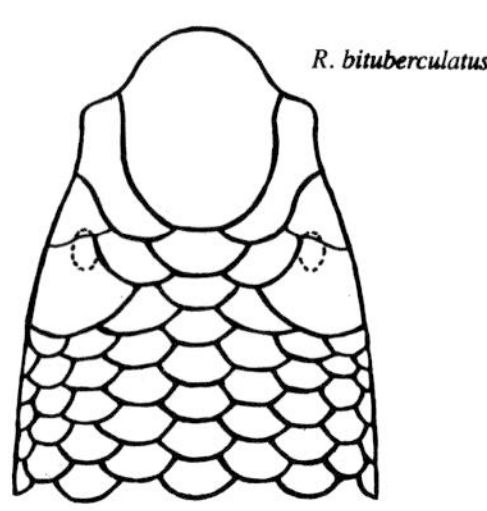

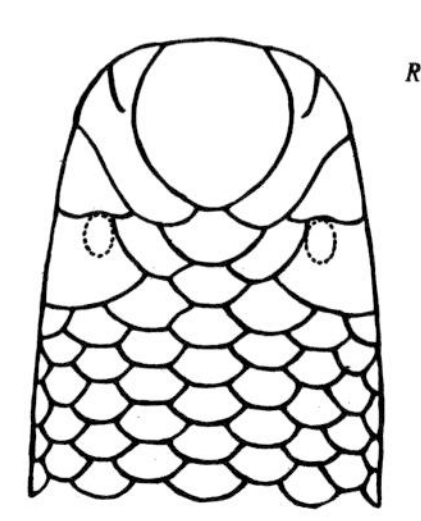

Worm Snakes
Genus *Ramphotyphlops*

All South-Eastern species are similar in gross appearance, varying from pink to some hue of grey or brown. All are covered with smooth, overlapping scales and have bodies that are absolutely cylindrical in shape, with both ends of the body ending quite suddenly; the tail being the end with a small conical spur at the tip; the head being the end without the spur, but usually with a regularly flickering tongue and moving forwards. The eyes appear only as reduced dark spots protected beneath transluscent scales. Average 0.2-0.3 m (0.12 m at hatching; maximum 0.3-0.7 m)

Worm Snakes are very secretive burrowing snakes that are usually found beneath stones or fallen timber. Most species are believed to feed exclusively on ants and termites, especially the eggs, pupae and cocoons of these. Unable to bite if handled, the Worm Snake's defence includes poking with its tail spur and the excretion of a foul-smelling deterrent from the vent.

Additional information regarding Worm Snakes on page 9

Ramphotyphlops affinis

Both photographs S. Wilson)

Mark Hutchinson

Ramphotyphlops australis

Mark Hutchinson

Glenn Shea

Mark Hutchinson

Ramphotyphlops bituberculatus

Ramphotyphlops ligatus

Peter Robertson

Mark Hutchinson

Ramphotyphlops nigrescens

Mark Hutchinso

Peter Robertson

Peter Robertson

Ramphotyphlops proximus

Mark Hutchinson

Ramphotyphlops wiedii

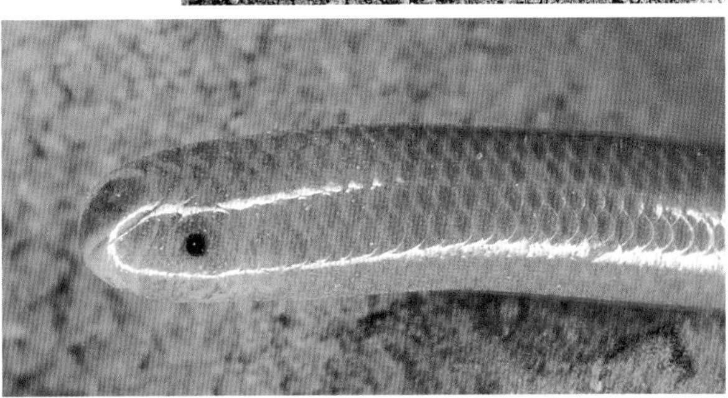

S. Wilson

Key to the Family Boidae (Pythons)

1 Scales on top of head large and shield-like ...***Liasis maculosus***
(Eastern Children's Python, page 27)

Scales on top of head small and granular **2**

shield-like head scales

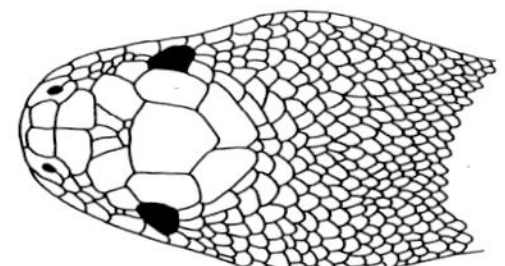

granular head scales

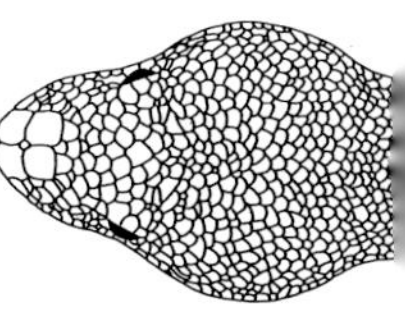

2 From coastal New South Wales or adjacent eastern slopes of Great Dividing Range south of the Northern Rivers District of northern New South Wales ....***Morelia spilota spilota***
(Diamond Python, pp 28, 29)

From the western slopes of the Great Dividing Range westwards, or north of the Northern Rivers District ....
....***Morelia spilota variegata***
(Carpet Python, pp 28, 29)

(note: These divisions into subspecies are arbitrary, and some specimens - especially from the Northern Rivers District of NSW are intermediate between the two 'types'.)

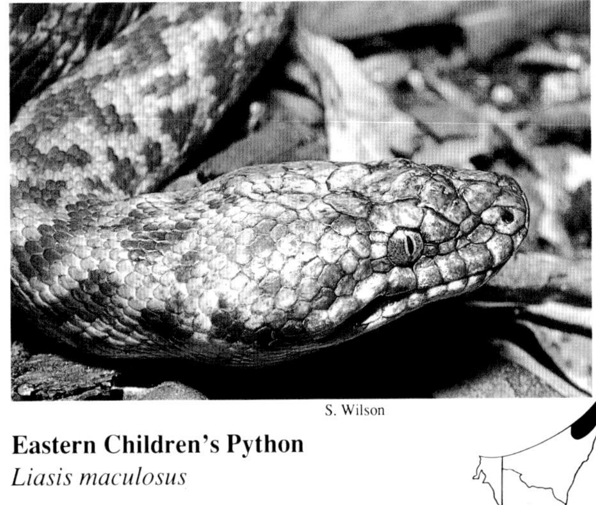

S. Wilson

Eastern Children's Python

Liasis maculosus

Small python with large head scales and small heat sensory pits along the lower jaw only. Cream to light brown above, largely obscured by numerous dark brown to purplish-brown splotches. Belly white. Differs from the Carpet/Diamond Python *Morelia spilota* by having large shield-like scales on head (vs small granular scales). Average 0.7 m (0.2 m at hatching; maximum 1.0 m).

Restricted to rocky areas where it emerges from crevices at night to lay upon sun-warmed stones or to pursue lizards and small mammals.

Additional information on page 10

. Wilson

Diamond and Carpet Pythons

Morelia spilota (refer also to following page)

This species includes two races or subspecies within the region, differing primarily in colouration. Both are large, heavily built snakes with numerous heat-sensory pits on upper and lower lips and small granular scales covering the head. Average for both subspecies is 1.8-2.0 m (0.4 m at hatching; maximum 3.0 m).

The Diamond Python and Carpet Python are largely arboreal and although widespread and common in heavily timbered country, they are secretive and seldom encountered - usually sheltering by day within hollow logs, rock crevices, dense vegetation, and occasionally, in rural barns and home attics. Mainly nocturnal; adults forage for mammals and birds at night, but may be found sun-basking during mornings or later during cool days. Juveniles are believed to prey largely upon lizards.

juvenile *M. s. spilota*

Mark Hutchinso

Peter Robertson

/lark Hutchinson

juvenile *M. s. variegata*

The Diamond Python *Morelia spilota spilota* (photos opposite page) is black or very dark brown above, heavily speckled with cream or yellow spots in patterned groups. Intensity of pattern and size of light spots is variable. Juveniles (to approximately 0.5 m) are typically dark or dull reddish-brown and drably marked. From Taree northwards, adults become increasingly drab while juveniles become more reddish.

The Carpet Python *Morelia spilota variegata* (photos this page) usually has broad alternating bands of lighter and darker shades of tan, brown or reddish-brown. Juveniles are usually reddish-brown. Coastal and inland populations differ in colouration as indicated in the photographs, while intermediate colour patterns occur in the intervening areas and there may be individual variants in any population. An intermediate 'intergrade' Diamond/Carpet Python exists in the Northern Rivers district of New South Wales.

Additional information on Carpet/Diamond Pythons on page 10

. Wilson

Key to the Family Colubridae (Colubrid Snakes)

1 Body scales rugose, each with a faint or distinct ridge or keel extending from base to tip .... ***Tropidonophis mairii***
(Keelback, page 32)
Body scales smooth **2**

2 Predominantly tan to reddish-brown above with darker blotches forming indistinct cross-bands, salmon or dull-yellow belly colouration; pupils vertically elliptical .... ***Boiga irregularis***
(Brown Tree Snake, page 30)
Drab-olive to green above, with bright yellow belly colouration extending to lower flanks; pupils round ....
.... ***Dendrelaphis punctulatus***
(Green Tree Snake, page 31)

Brown Tree Snake

Boiga irregularis

Body and tail whip-like; head very broad and distinct from narrow neck. The eyes are very large, with vertically elliptical pupils. Tan to reddish-brown above with darker cross-bands; belly cream to salmon. The Brown Tree Snake has a primitive venom apparatus and a mildly toxic venom. Average 1.2 metres (0.3 m at hatching; maximum 1.8 m).

Inhabits rock crevices or hollow branches by day, foraging at night for lizards, small mammals and birds. Inclined to bite if handled, but rarely producing symptoms of envenomation.

Additional information on page 10; additional photo back cover

Grant Husband

Green Tree Snake

Dendrelaphis punctulatus

Very elongate body, with long and narrow head. Some shade of green or olive above, with top of head usually darker. Belly canary-yellow; this vivid colour extends upwards to lower flanks and from chin upwards to eye level. When excited, the Green Tree Snake may inflate itself to expose yellow skin that is otherwise hidden between overlapped scales. Although harmless, care should be taken that the dangerously venomous Eastern Brown Snake *Pseudonaja textilis* is not confused with this species. The Green Tree Snake has loreal scales, the Brown Snake does not (see figure on page 16).

This diurnal, arboreal species is commonly encountered in well timbered areas, sheltering in hollow branches and rock crevices. It may enter homes through any available gap in search of its favourite prey - frogs. Average 1.2 metres (0.25 m at hatching; maximum 1.8 m).

Additional information on page 10, 83

Mark Hutchinson

Mark Hutchinson

Keelback

Tropidonophis mairii

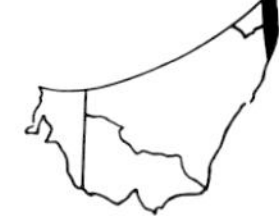

Colour variable; olive, brown, reddish-brown, or light to very dark grey. Lighter coloured specimens are often peppered with dark spots. Belly cream, olive or salmon. Each body scale has a faint to distinct ridge or keel transecting it from base to tip creating a rough texture to the skin. Although harmless, the Keelback may be confused with the dangerously venomous Rough-scaled Snake *Tropidechis carinatus*. In the Keelback, the scales along the neck and body are proportionately broader than in the Rough-scaled Snake, and the head is shorter and flatter. The Keelback has loreal scales (see figure on page 16) and 15-17 rows of scales around the middle of the body while the Rough-scale Snake has 23.

Usually found in close proximity to water where it feeds primarily on frogs at night, resting by day beneath fallen timber and other debris. A pugnacious species, if handled it may bite. Average 0.5 m (0.15 m at hatching; maximum 0.8 m).

Additional information on page 10

Key to the Family Elapidae (Front-fanged, Venomous Snakes)

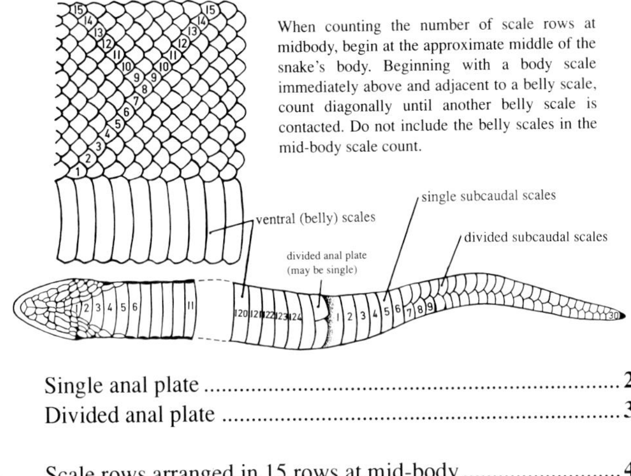

When counting the number of scale rows at midbody, begin at the approximate middle of the snake's body. Beginning with a body scale immediately above and adjacent to a belly scale, count diagonally until another belly scale is contacted. Do not include the belly scales in the mid-body scale count.
single subcaudal scales
ventral (belly) scales
divided subcaudal scales
divided anal plate (may be single)

1 Single anal plate **2**
Divided anal plate **3**

2 Scale rows arranged in 15 rows at mid-body **4**
Scale rows arranged in 17 or more rows at mid-body **12**

3 Scale rows arranged in 15 rows at mid-body **26**
Scale rows arranged in 17 or more rows at mid-body **33**

4

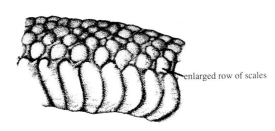

enlarged row of scales

The first row of body scales to either side of the belly scales noticably enlarged and lighter coloured than those above; markings on upper lip (if any) confined to narrow to wide, vertically or diagonally oriented white bars or triangles .... ***Austrelaps superbus***
(Copperhead, pp 42-44)

No row of enlarged body scales just above belly scales; if white or cream markings occur on upper lip they are oriented horizontally or lip is entirely white or cream **5**

5 Body and head (including upper lip) are uniformly black or very dark grey above, (occasionally body is blue-grey above while head is black), in either case glossy and often with a bluish tint .... ***Cryptophis nigrescens***
(Small-eyed Snake, page 48)

Predominantly brown above; otherwise, with at least some light colouration on upper lip **6**

6 A broad pale or reddish band extends across nape **7**
No pale or reddish band extends across nape **8**

7 Specimen from South Australia or western Victoria; lip stripe present .... ***Drysdalia mastersii***
(Masters' Snake, page 54)

Specimen from eastern New South Wales; lip stripe absent .....
.... ***Drysdalia rhodogaster***
(Rose-bellied Whip Snake, page 55)

8 Top of head black **9**
Top of head tan, brown or reddish brown **11**

9 Dark vertebral stripe extending the length of the body; top of head black usually without interruption by a light coloured patch just before eye; from South Australia, Victoria or southwestern New South Wales .... ***Unechis nigriceps***
(Southern Black-striped Snake, page 80)

Top of head black, interupted or completely divided by light-coloured patch between eye and nostril. No vertebral stripe (except rarely in specimens from within 200 km of the Queensland and New South Wales border) **10**

10 From South Australia, western Victoria, or far western New South Wales (west of the Darling River) ... ***Unechis spectabilis***
(no common name, page 81)

From Queensland, eastern Victoria, or New South Wales (if more than 150 kms east of the South Australian border) ....
.... ***Unechis dwyeri***
(Dwyer's Snake, page 78)

11 Subcaudal scales number 20-35; from Queensland or adjacent border of New South Wales .... ***Unechis boschmai*** (Carpentaria Snake, page 77)

Subcaudal scales number 35-70; from Victoria or highland New South Wales .... ***Drysdalia coronoides*** (White-lipped Snake, page 53)

12 Scale rows arranged in 17 or 19 rows at mid-body **13**
Scale rows arranged in 21 or more rows at mid-body **19**

13 Subcaudal scales all divided..................... ***Simoselaps australis*** (Coral Snake, page 74)
Subcaudal scales single **14**

14

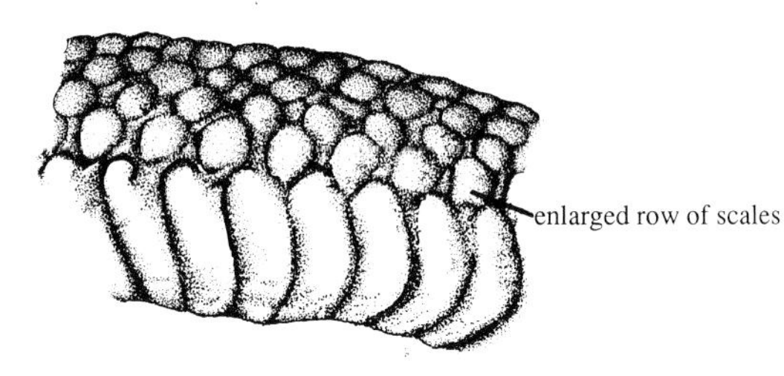

First row of body scales to either side of the belly scales noticably enlarged and lighter coloured than those above; markings on upper lip (if any) are confined to narrow to wide, vertically or diagonally oriented white bars or triangles; 17 rows of scales at mid-body .... ***Austrelaps superbus*** (Copperhead, pp 42-44)

No row of enlarged and lighter coloured body scales just above belly scales; markings on upper lip (of any nature) may or may not be present; 17 or 19 rows of scales at mid-body **15**

15 Upper lip and/or snout with some form of distinct light and/or dark streaks, lines, flecks or bars; if top of head is black, contrasting markings may consist only of a sharply defined tan, cream or white zone on upper lip, possibly extending above eye-level **16**

No distinct light and/or dark streaks, lines, flecks, bars, or sharply defined lighter coloured zone on upper lip and/or snout **18**

16 Body scales arranged in 17 rows at mid-body **17**
Body scales arranged in 19 or more rows at mid-body **19**

17 Body light brown to reddish-brown above with numerous dark irregular cross-bands .... ***Denisonia devisii*** (De Vis' Banded Snake, page 51)

Apart from fine reticulations that may be present if individual scales have narrow dark edges, body uniformly coloured without numerous cross-bands .... ***Unechis flagellum*** (Little Whip Snake, page 79)

18 From Tasmania or other off-shore island (or from Flinders Range or southern half of Yorke Peninsula, South Australia) ***Notechis ater*** (Black Tiger Snake, page 63)

From Australian mainland, but not from Flinders Ranges or southern Yorke Peninsula, South Australia ..***Notechis scutatus*** (Common Tiger Snake, pp 64,65)

19 Subcaudal scales all (or at least mostly) single **20**
Subcaudal scales all divided .... ***Oxyuranus scutellatus*** (Taipan, page 66)

20

modified tail tip

Tail laterally compressed (flattened from side to side) terminating with a tiny soft spine .... ***Acanthophis antarcticus*** (Death Adder, page 41)

Tail not laterally compressed (flattened from side to side) nor terminating with a tiny soft spine **21**

21 Subcaudal scales number 20-39 .... **22**
Subcaudal scales number 40 or more **23**

22 White, cream, yellow or light brown stripe extends from snout, through eye to temple .... ***Denisonia suta***
(Curl Snake, page 52)

Upper lip marked only with white flecks or vertically oriented bars; not with horizontal stripe .... ***Echiopsis curta***
(Bardick, page 56)

23 Each body scale with a faint to distinct ridge or keel transecting it from base to tip creating a rough texture to the skin ....
.... ***Tropidechis carinatus***
(Rough-scaled Snake, page 76)

Body scales smooth **24**

24 Body uniformly grey to dark grey above; broad pale blotch over nape, bordered behind by narrow black bar which may be fragmented .... ***Hoplocephalus bitorquatus***
(Pale-headed Snake, page 60)

Body with cream or yellow cross-bands or with yellow spots; no broad pale blotch over nape **25**

25 Black above with series of bright yellow dots usually forming thin irregular cross-bands and often zig-zagging along lower sides of body .... ***Hoplocephalus bungaroides***
(Broad-headed Snake, page 61)

Black above, usually with yellowish-brown cross-bands two or more scales wide; if no bands, head is primarily black above eye level, not pale-grey mottled with dark spots) ....
.... ***Hoplocephalus stephensi***
(Stephen's Banded Snake, page 62)

26 Bright orange or red blotch on nape interrupting otherwise uniformly glossy black top of head and neck ....
.... ***Furina diadema***
(Red-naped Snake, page 57)

No bright orange or red blotch on nape surrounded by glossy black **27**

27 Subcaudal scales number less than 55 .... **28**
Subcaudal scales number more than 55 .... **29**

28 Alternating broad black bands around or across body **30**
No alternating broad black bands around or across body **31**

29 A narrow, white-edged, dark line horizontally crosses tip of snout .... ***Demansia psammophis***
(Yellow-faced Whip Snake, page 50)

No white-edged, dark line horizontally crosses tip of snout...... .... ***Demansia atra***
(Black Whip Snake, page 49)

30 Body coloration consists entirely of alternating black and white rings around body .... ***Vermicella annulata***
(Bandy Bandy, page 82)

Body colouration includes yellow or orange .... ***Simoselaps bertholdii***
(Desert Banded Snake, page 75)

31 Belly evenly dark grey .... ***Cacophis harrietae***
(White-crowned Snake, page 45)

Belly not evenly dark grey **32**

32 Belly cream with darker edges to belly scales; cream or yellow bar extends completely across nape .... ***Cacophis krefftii***
(Krefft's Dwarf Snake, page 46)

Belly red, orange or pink, usually interrupted with dark spots; markings on top of neck are bayish, dull yellow or gold and do not (except very rarely) form a complete band across nape .... ***Cacophis squamulosus***
(Golden-crowned Snake, page 47)

33 Ventral scales number 140-174 (or as many as 175, if subcaudal scales all divided).. **34**

Ventral scales number 176-235 (or as few as175, if first few subcaudal scales from vent single) **36**

34 Subcaudal scales number fewer than 32 .. ***Simoselaps australis***
(Coral Snake, page 74)

Subcaudal scales number more than 32 .... **35**

35 Subcaudal scales all divided .... ***Pseudonaja modesta***
(Five-ringed Snake, page 70)

First few subcaudal scales from vent are single or all subcaudal scales are single **36**

36 Subcaudal scales all single; no pink or red margin visible along the lower margin of the body **37**

Subcaudal scales all divided, or with the first few from vent single (if all subcaudals single, body glossy-black above with pink or red margin visible along the lower margin of the body) **38**

37 Two white to yellow streaks extend across the face; one along upper lip, the other from the eye towards the neck .... ***Hemiaspis signata***
(Swamp Snake, page 59)

No light coloured streaks across upper lip or face .... ***Hemiaspis damelii***
(Grey Snake, page 58)

38 Body glossy-black above with pink or red margin visible along the lower margin of the body .... ***Pseudechis porphyriacus***
(Red-bellied Black Snake, page 69)

Body other than glossy-black above, or, if glossy black above; then without pink or red margin visible along the lower margin of the body **39**

39 Presence of inverted pyramid-shaped lower temporal scale interrupting upper labial scales **40**

No inverted pyramid-shaped lower temporal scale interupting upper labial scales **41**

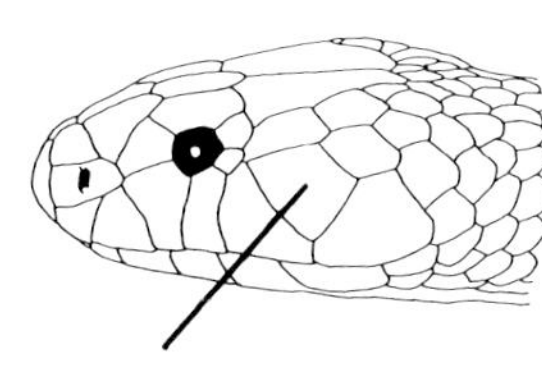

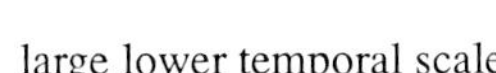

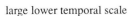

large lower temporal scale

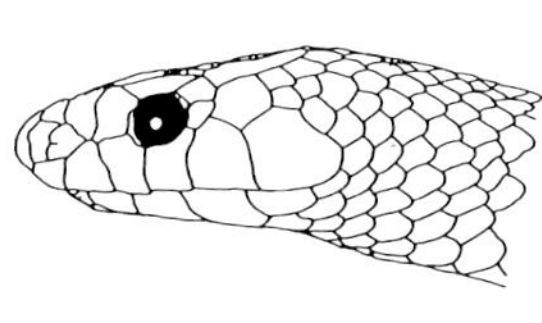

no lower temporal scale

40 Usually with at least a few dark flecks or blotches over nape or neck. Sometimes with distinct cross-bands at least several scales wide across body; rostral (snout) scale enlarged and strap-like; inside lining of mouth black .... ***Pseudonaja nuchalis*** (Western Brown Snake, page 71)

If larger than 0.5 m, no pattern of dark pigmentation above, except occasionally where obscure and narrow (no more than two scales wide) dark cross-bands exist, and rarely, where a vague dark zone extends over head and/or nape. In juvenile specimens (to 0.5 m) strongly defined narrow dark bands may be present. Rostral (snout) scale not enlarged and strap-like. Inside lining of mouth pink .... ***Pseudonaja textilis*** (Eastern Brown Snake, pp 72,73)

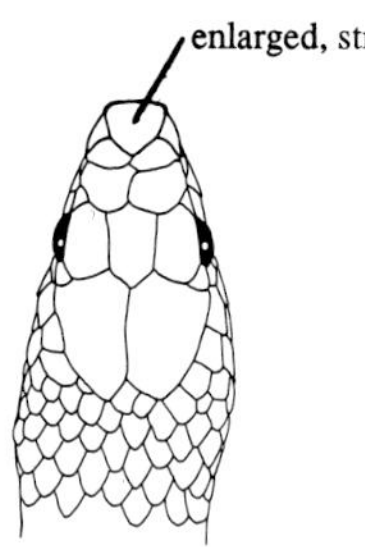

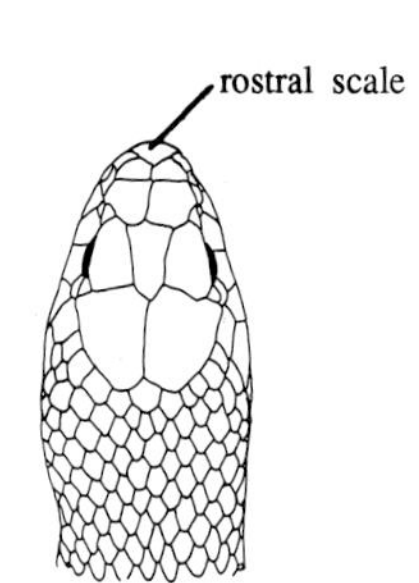

41 Body scales in 17 rows at mid-body .... ***Pseudechis australis*** (King Brown Snake, page 67)

Body scales in 19 rows at mid-body .... ***Pseudechis guttatus*** (Spotted Black Snake, page 68)

Robert Cook

Death Adder

Acanthophis antarcticus

dangerously venomous

Very robust snake with broad head distinct from neck; head and neck scales at least mildly rugose. The short tail has at its tip a flattened section terminating in a soft spine (rarely, this portion of tail is lost through injury). Colour above is variable, being light or dark grey, brown or reddish; usually with lighter and darker cross-bands. Belly is white.

The Death Adder hides amongst leaf litter or beneath low shrubs, from where it ambushes lizards and other small animals. Occasionally moves about during warm nights or overcast, warm days. If tormented, it flattens its body and may lash about wildly in an attempt to bite. Average 0.6 m (0.18 m at birth; maximum 0.9 m).

Additional information on pp 12, 89, 93

ter Robertson

Mark Hutchinson

Copperhead

Austrelaps superbus

dangerously venomous

(photographs pp 42-44)

Stout-bodied snake with unusual condition of having the first row of body scales to either side of the belly noticably enlarged and usually lighter coloured than those above. Colouration varies from grey to dull smokey-black, reddish-brown or brassy above, often with dull reddish-orange or yellow along the lower sides; markings on upper lip (if any) are confined to vertically or diagonally orientied white bars or triangles. Some specimens possess a dark vertebral stripe running the length of body. In lighter coloured specimens the head may be dark and there may be a dark band across the neck. Body is never banded. Belly is cream to grey often with a black edge along each belly scale. Some published accounts distinguish three different forms of Copperhead, the 'highlands' race, the 'lowlands' race and the 'pygmy' race, though these have not been traditionally accepted as different species.

The highlands form (photos this page only) inhabits moist alpine and subalpine habitats in NSW and the Victorian highlands. It is usually a dark brown to smokey black above. Average 0.6 m (0.15 m at birth; maximum 1.2 m)

Additional information for Copperheads on pp 14, 89, 93

Mark Hutchinso

ark Hutchinson

Well watered environments at lower altitude provide the habitat for the lowlands form of the Copperhead (photos this page only), which is of a lighter colouration than the highlands form, usually being brownish-orange to brassy above. Average 1.0 m (0.15 m at birth; max 1.6 m).

ark Hutchinson

Glenn Shea

The pygmy form of Copperhead (photos this page only) attains a length of about 0.5 m and occurs only in the Mt. Lofty Range of South Australia and on nearby Kangaroo Island. Pale brown or light to dark grey above. Specimens over 0.6 m are rare.

Mark Hutchinsc

ary Stephenson

White-crowned Snake
Cacophis harriettae

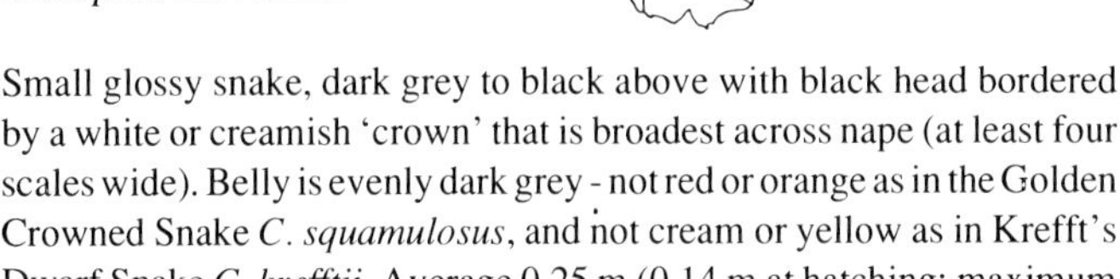

Small glossy snake, dark grey to black above with black head bordered by a white or creamish 'crown' that is broadest across nape (at least four scales wide). Belly is evenly dark grey - not red or orange as in the Golden Crowned Snake *C. squamulosus*, and not cream or yellow as in Krefft's Dwarf Snake *C. krefftii*. Average 0.25 m (0.14 m at hatching; maximum 0.4 m).

Inhabits moist, forested areas but is often found in suburban gardens. Nocturnal, resting by day beneath logs, stones etc. When threatened, the head is raised and mock strikes (with mouth closed) are directed at the perceived danger. Feeds mainly upon small skinks.

bert Cook

Peter Robertson

Krefft's Dwarf Snake
Cacophis krefftii

Small glossy snake, brownish-black to greyish-black above with black head bordered by a pale 'crown'. Where the crown extends across the nape, it is usually yellow and only one or two scales wide. Where it extends through eye and across snout, it may be cream and somewhat broken up. The underside is cream with darker edges to belly and tail scales. Differs from other *Cacophis* species by nature of crown and colour of belly. Average 0.2 m (0.12 m at hatching; maximum 0.3 m).

Inhabits moist, forested areas but is often found in suburban gardens. Nocturnal, resting by day beneath logs, stones etc. When threatened, the head is raised and mock strikes (with mouth closed) are directed at the perceived danger. Feeds mainly upon small skinks.

Peter Robertson

S. Wilson

Golden-crowned Snake
Cacophis squamulosus

Small glossy snake, yellowish-brown, dark brown or dark greyish-brown above with a dark head that is partially bordered by a pale 'crown' extending across the snout and through the eye along sides of face, where it is usually cream. Rather than joining across the nape, the two sides of the crown extend in tandem a short distance along the neck, where they are usually yellowish-brown to gold. Belly red, orange or pink, usually interrupted with dark spots. Differs from other *Cacophis* species by nature of crown and colour of belly. Average 0.35 m (0.2 m at hatching; maximum 0.6 m).

Inhabits moist, forested areas but is often found in suburban gardens. Nocturnal, resting by day beneath logs, stones etc. When threatened, the head is raised and mock strikes (with mouth closed) are directed at the perceived danger. Feeds mainly upon small skinks.

Gary Stephenson

Mark Hutchinson

Glenn Shea

Mark Hutchinsc

Small-eyed Snake

Cryptophis nigrescens

potentially dangerous species

This small glossy snake has small, dark and inconspicuous eyes. It is uniformly coloured above - usually black, less commonly dark grey, and sometimes with a bluish tint. The belly scales are evenly pink or reddish but may be light grey, cream or blue-black. If red, this pigment does not extend upward to the lower sides of the snake as it does in the Red-bellied Black Snake *Pseudechis porphyriacus* (in which the red is confined mainly to the lower lateral scales just *above* the belly scales, while the belly scales themselves are dark on the outer edges and yellowish in the centre). Average 0.3 m (0.18 m at birth; maximum 0.7 m).

The Small-eyed Snake is nocturnal, and feeds primarily upon lizards and snakes. Usually found by day, resting beneath flat stones or loose bark of fallen trees. Also frequently encountered moving across roads at night. Able to deliver a nasty bite if handled; bite victims should seek medical attention.

S. Wilson

Black Whip Snake

Demansia atra

potentially dangerous species

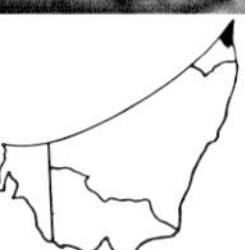

Slender bodied snake with narrow head. Olive-brown to reddish-brown above. Belly is white from chin to base of tail, wherafter it often takes on a reddish hue. Differs from similarly built, more dangerously venomous species by having only 15 scale rows at mid-body. May be distinguished from the Yellow-faced Whip Snake *D. psammophis*, by lacking a narrow white-edged, dark line across the tip of the snout. Average 1.0 m (0.2 m at hatching; maximum 1.5 m).

This very active diurnal snake preys upon lizards, which it chases at high speed. Prefers dry, sandy country where it shelters beneath stones, logs and other debris when inactive. Bites from large specimens should be regarded as potentially serious.

Wilson

Mark Hutchinsc

Yellow-faced Whip Snake

Demansia psammophis

A very elongate snake with a narrow head. Greyish or olive above, usually with a flush of salmon or red extending along the upper flanks of the first third of the body. A black "comma" slopes downwards from the back of the eye to the lip edge, and is normally bordered on either side with yellow. A narrow, white edged, dark line extends across front of snout; this is absent in *D. atra*. A distinct subspecies *D. p. reticulata* (pictured above right) is present in the Flinders Ranges of South Australia and further west, differing from *D. p. psammophis* in having each body scale margined with black giving rise to a distinct reticulated pattern. Average 0.8 m (0.2 m at hatching; maximum 1.2 m).

Similar in habit to the Black Whip Snake *D. atra*. The Yellow-faced Whip Snake is one of the most commonly encountered snakes throughout its range, and though not aggressive may bite if handled, resulting in extreme pain along the affected limb.

Additional information on page 85

Mark Hutchins

De Vis' Banded Snake

Denisonia devisii

potentially dangerous species

A short, squat snake similar in form to the Death Adder *Acanthophis antarcticus*, from which it differs by lacking a modified, spinous tail tip and rugose head scalation. Light brown or reddish-brown above with numerous darker irregular cross-bands; top of head is same dark colour. Belly colour cream. Average 0.35 m (0.15 m at birth; maximum 0.6 m).

Usually found in areas of relatively thick vegetation. It is nocturnal and eats frogs and geckos. If handled or otherwise molested, this snake becomes very pugnacious and will thrash about in an attempt to bite.

Additional information on page 12

Mark Hutchinson

lenn Shea

Curl Snake

Denisonia suta

potentially dangerous species

Various shades of brown to reddish-brown above. Top of head blackish or brown (which fades with age), interrupted on each side by a light cream, yellow or light brown stripe extending from snout, through eye to temple, and a white irregular streak along upper lip and narrowly, across front of snout. Belly is white or cream. While the body scales often have dark tips creating a reticulating pattern, the body is not strongly banded as in *D. devisii*. Body scales are in 19 rows at mid-body (vs 17 for *D. devisii* and *Hemiaspis*, 15 for *Unechis* and *Drysdalia* species). Average 0.4 m (0.15 m at birth; maximum 0.6 m).

The Curl Snake is a nocturnal, skink-eating species. When alarmed it may flail about madly in an attempt to bite.

Additional information on page 11

Robert Cook

Mark Hutchinsc

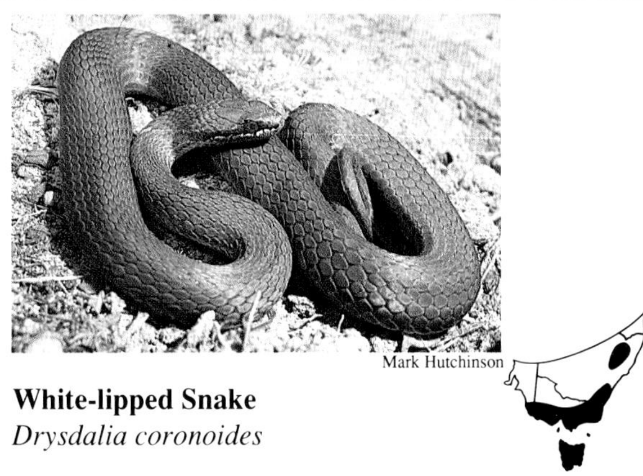

Mark Hutchinson

White-lipped Snake
Drysdalia coronoides

Colouration above may be of various shades of grey, brown or reddish-brown (juveniles are black), often finely peppered with pink; always with a narrow white streak along the upper lip margined above by a dark streak that passes through the eye. There is no band across the nape nor any white vertical barring on upper lip. Belly cream, yellow or pink. The White-lipped Snake can be distinguished from the Swamp Snake *Hemiaspis signata* by having 15 scale rows at mid-body (vs 17), and in not having a grey or black belly. Average 0.35 m (0.13 m at birth; maximum 0.5 m).

This species inhabits mountainous forests and water-soaked areas, often in proximity to the Copperhead. It can be active by day or night, but is commonly found hidden beneath logs or stones. Feeds principally upon small skinks. Will bite if handled.

'ark Hutchinson

Peter Robertson

Masters Snake

Drysdalia mastersii

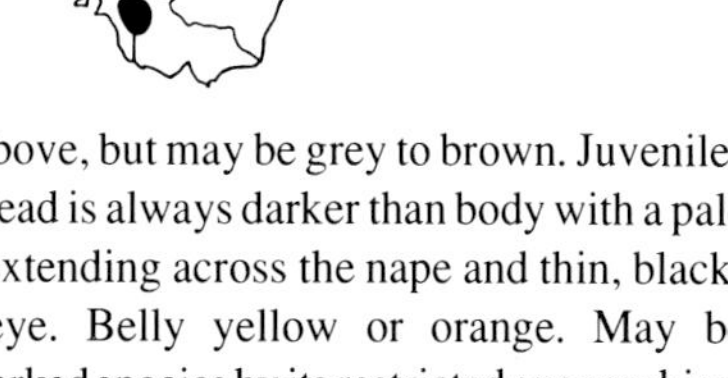

Usually predominantly olive above, but may be grey to brown. Juveniles tend to be darker than adults. Head is always darker than body with a pale band (often yellowish to red) extending across the nape and thin, black-edged, white streak under eye. Belly yellow or orange. May be distinguished from similarly marked species by its restricted geographical distribution. Differs from the White-lipped Snake *D. coronoides* by having a pale bar across nape. Average 0.35 m (0.12 m at birth; maximum 0.4 m).

Inhabits semi-arid plains, sandy hills and coastal dunes. Principally diurnal but is commonly found hidden in grass tussocks or low dense shrubs or beneath logs or stones. Feeds principally upon small skinks.

Mark Hutchinso

Rose-bellied Whip Snake
Drysdalia rhodogaster

Olive to brown above, often very finely peppered with pink. Head black on top but mottled with cream colouration over snout and sides of face. A narrow black stripe extends from the nostril to the eye. A prominent orange to light brown band crosses the nape. Belly yellow to orange. Differs from *D. coronoides* and *Hemiaspis signata* in bearing a pale band across nape, and in lacking a distinct narrow white stripe along upper lip. Average 0.3 m (0.13 m at hatching; maximum 0.45 m).

This species is most active by day, and like most small elapid snakes, it is often found resting beneath warm sheets of discarded metal and other refuse. Feeds mainly upon skinks.

Alex Dudley

eter Robertson

Peter Robertson

Bardick

Echiopsis curta

potentially dangerous species

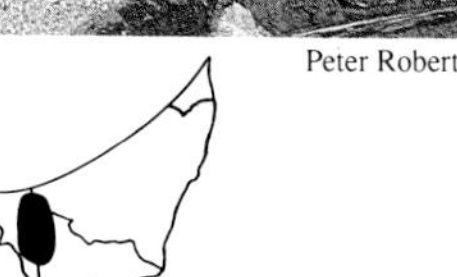

Moderately robust species with broad head. Olive to dark grey-brown above. Side of head and neck usually flecked with white. Belly pale grey or cream. Differs from the Curl Snake *Denisonia suta* and the Master's Snake *D. mastersii* by lacking light or dark streak through (or just below) eye, from snout to angle of jaws. Differs from the Death Adder *Acanthophis antarcticus*, by lacking a modified, spinous tail tip and rugose head scalation. Average 0.3 m (0.13 m at birth; maximum 0.6 m).

Favours sandy Mallee woodlands where it hides amongst fallen leaf litter, amongst grass tussocks and beneath shrubs. Active by day or night preying principally on lizards. It is inclined to bite savagely if provoked, resulting in extreme pain and discomfort.

H. G. Cogger

S. Wilson

Red-naped Snake
Furina diadema

Background colour cream along flanks, usually becoming reddish towards top of body. Usually each body scale is outlined with a narrow black margin, yielding an overall reticulated pattern above. Head and neck shiny black above without any lighter markings on lips or face, but with a distinctive red, cresent-shaped mark extending across nape. The eyes are small, black and difficult to discern. Belly white or cream. May be confused with juvenile Eastern Brown Snake *Pseudonaja textilis*, though the latter has much larger eyes and pale markings on upper lip. Average 0.3 m (0.12 m at hatching; maximum 0.5 m).

Commonly found beneath rocks and logs, especially amongst rocky outcrops. Preys on small lizards.

S. Wilson

Robert Cook

Grey Snake

Hemiaspis damelii

Grey to olive-brown above, sometimes with a dark spot at the base of each scale. Head is black in young specimens, but this colour fades with age to become a broad band across the nape, or the dark colour may disappear entirely. Belly is cream but may be lightly flecked with grey. Differs from both the Curl Snake *Denisonia suta* and the White-lipped Snake *Drysdalia coronoides* by lacking any distinct horizontally oriented white streak along upper lip and across snout. Differs from *Hoplocephalus bitorquatus* and *Echiopsis curta* in having a divided anal plate. Differs from juvenile Spotted Black Snake *Pseudechis guttatus* in having 17 vs 19 rows of scales at mid-body. Average 0.4 m (0.15 m at birth; maximum 0.6 m).

Mainly active during warm evenings, feeding primarily on frogs.

S. Wilson

Swamp Snake
Hemiaspis signata

Olive to dark brown or black above. Two white to yellow streaks extend across the face; one extending along the upper lip from snout to angle of jaw, the other from the eye towards the neck. Belly grey to nearly black. Differs from *D. coronoides* and *D. suta* in having a divided anal plate. Average 0.3 m (0.15 m at birth; maximum 0.5 m).

Active by day or on warm nights. Usually occurs in marshy areas, but is also commonly found in suburban yards where it shelters beneath timber, grass clipping or any other debris. Preys upon frogs and small skinks.

Gary Stephenson

Pale-headed Snake
Hoplocephalus bitorquatus
potentially dangerous species

Light grey to dark grey above. Head broad, flat and mottled with black spots. These black spots may also be present on lips and neck. A broad pale blotch lies over the nape and is bordered behind by a narrow black bar which may be fragmented. Belly cream to light grey, sometimes flecked with darker colour. Differs from unanded specimens of *Hoplocephalus stephensii* by presence of pale blotch over nape. Average 0.4 m (0.25 m at birth; maximum 1.0 m).

Inhabits forests and woodlands where it is reputed to shelter beneath loose tree bark. Nocturnal and at least partially arboreal, it preys mainly upon frogs.

Peter Robertson

Grant Husband

Broad-headed Snake

Hoplocephalus bungaroides
potentially dangerous species

Black above with series of yellow dots usually forming thin irregular cross-bands which may fuse to a zig-zag or solid yellow zone along the lower body, just above the belly. Belly is light or dark grey. Differs from the Diamond Python *Morelia spilota* by having large shield-like scales over the head (vs small granular scales). Head broad and flat. Differs from the Stephen's Banded Snake *H. stephensi* by having narrower cross-bands (usually only one scale wide vs two or more) Average 0.5 m (0.25 m at birth; maximum 1.0 m).

Occurs amongst sandstone ridges where it often shelters beneath flat rock exfoliations. Chiefly nocturnal, it preys upon lizards and frogs. Will bite if handled, resulting in extreme discomfort and illness.

Additional information on page 12

Robert Cook

Stephen's Banded Snake
Hoplocephalus stephensii
potentially dangerous species

Black or dark brown above, usually with yellowish brown cross-bands two or more scales wide, but in areas where its range of distribution overlaps with that of the Pale-headed Snake *H. bitorquatus*, occasional unbanded (possibly intergrade) specimens arise. Differs from most broadly banded species by having 21 rows of scales at mid-body. Head broad and flat. Average 0.5 m (0.25 m at birth; maximum 1.0 m).

This species inhabits well forested areas with high rainfall. It is mainly nocturnal and at least partially arboreal, sheltering by day within hollow branches and rock crevices, but is also known to sun-bask on occasion. Will bite if handled, resulting in extreme pain and some illness. Feeds upon lizards, birds and small mammals.

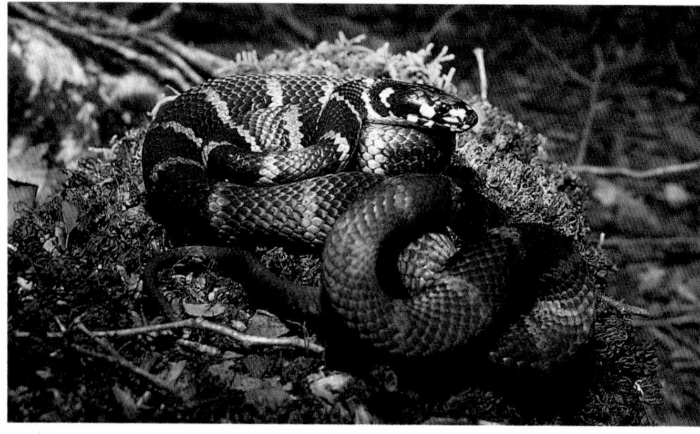

Mark Hutchinson

Black Tiger Snake

Notechis ater

dangerously venomous

Numerous subspecies of the Black Tiger Snake occur in the South-East. Colour is usually glossy black above, sometimes with faint, narrow cross-bands that may be reduced with age to only the lower flanks. In Tasmania and other islands, may be lighter coloured, sometimes with strong bands. The body is robust and the head is very broad. Belly colouration usually pale to dark grey. Average 0.8-1.2 m (0.2 m at birth; maximum 1.5-1.9 m).

The Black Tiger Snake is mainly diurnal, and feeds upon frogs, lizards and small mammals and birds.

S. Wilson

Mark Hutchinson

Comon Tiger Snake

Notechis scutatus

dangerously venomous

(additional photos opposite)

Large, robust snake, varying from grey to olive, tan, brown, reddish-brown or almost black above, usually with narrow to broad, lighter coloured cross-bands. Belly varies from cream to yellow to various shades of olive and grey. Banded specimens are easily identifiable, and unbanded specimens can be distinguised from other large Elapid snakes on the basis of scale conditions. Differs from the Copperhead *Austrelaps superba* by lacking row of enlarged scales on either side of belly scale row and in possessing 17-19 midbody scale rows vs almost always 15, very rarely 17. Juvenile Tiger Snakes may be distinguished from *Drysdalia* species by having 17-19 vs 15 mid-body scale rows; from all *Hemiaspis, Pseudechis* and *Pseudonaja* species by having a single (vs divided) anal plate and in having *all* single subcaudal scales. Average 1.0 m (0.18 at birth; maximum 1.8 m).

A diurnal sun-loving species usually associated with well-watered areas with abundant tussock grasses, especially just beyond the edges of swamps. Also in proximity to streams in rocky or well-timbered areas. Distribution extends far inland along banks of major river systems. Eats frogs, lizards, nestling water birds and mice. If provoked or stepped on will become very defensive and will not hesitate to bite.

Additional information on pp 13, 89, 93

Mark Hutchinson

Mark Hutchinson

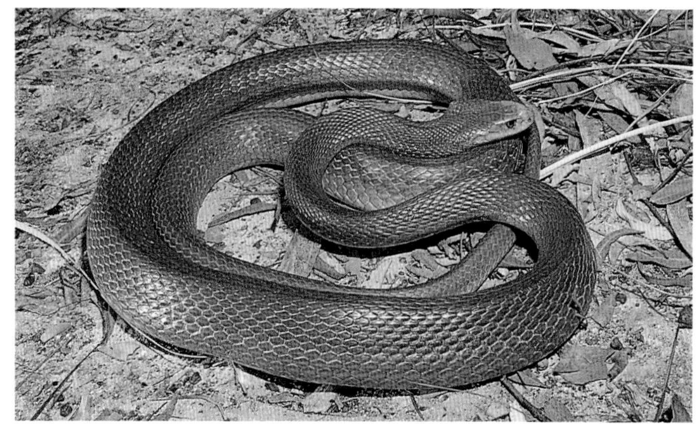

Taipan

Oxyuranus scutellatus

dangerously venomous

Large snake with a long and narrow, coffin-shaped head. May be tan, yellowish-brown, light or dark brown (to almost black) or brassy above; usually lighter on top of head, or at least along snout and sides of face. Belly cream or pale yellow with scattered orange spots or blotches. The Taipan is rare in the South-East; most reports prove to be misidentified Common Brown Snakes *Pseudonaja textilis*, from which it differs in having a greater number of scale rows at mid-body (21-23 vs 17). Average 1.8 m (0.45 m at hatching; maximum 2.4 m).

Feeds exclusively on rodents and other small mammals. An alert and very fast moving diurnal species, the Taipan is likely to avoid approaching humans on most occasions. However, if startled or cornered, it may strike repeatedly with deadly speed and accuracy.

Additional information on pp 13, 86, 89, 93

S. Wilson

Peter Robertson

King Brown or Mulga Snake
Pseudechis australis
dangerously venomous

A large, heavily built snake with a broad flat head (vs narrow and 'coffin-shaped' in *Pseudonaja*). Light to dark brown (to nearly black), brassy or reddish-brown above. Scales may be dark-edged, resulting in a distinct reticulated pattern. Belly uniform cream to yellow, occasionally with scattered orange blotches. Differs from the Eastern Brown Snake *Pseudonaja textilis* and the Western Brown Snake *Pseudonaja nuchalis* by having a large lower temporal scale (see figure on page 39). Average 1.3-1.8 m; males larger than females (0.25 m at hatching; maximum 2.2 m).

This widespread inhabitant of arid districts is active during warm evenings, or by day during the cooler months. It is relatively slow moving and placid, and unlikely to bite unless handled or otherwise abused. Eats practically any animal that it is able to overpower and swallow, including other species of snakes. *Additional information on pp 13, 89, 93*

Mark Hutchinson

Spotted or Blue-bellied Black Snake

Pseudechis guttatus

dangerously venomous

A robust snake with relatively flat head indistinct from neck. May be black, grey, light brown, cream or reddish-brown above, with or without a pale spot in the centre of each body scale. Juveniles paler than adults. Belly colour varies from cream to grey to blue-black. Cream or light reddish-brown specimens usually have black-tipped body scales, darker head than body colouration and cream to light grey bellies. Distinguishable from the Red-bellied Black Snake *P. porphyriacus* by lacking red or pink colouration along lower flanks. Differs from the King Brown Snake *P. australis* and most other snake species by having 19 rows of scales at midbody. Average 0.8-1.2 m; males larger than females (0.2 m at hatching; maximum 1.8 m).

A fairly shy species that if provoked flattens its body and hisses, biting only as a final resort. Active mainly by day, feeding on mice, frogs and lizards.

Additional information on pp 13, 89

Greg Parker

Mark Hutchinson

Red-bellied Black Snake

Pseudechis porphyriacus

dangerously venomous

Glossy black above, with a flash of red or pink visible along the lower margin of the body, just above ground level. The centre of the belly is mainly dull yellowish. The unique colouration of the Red-bellied Black Snake makes identification straightforward. Average 1.0-1.5 m; males larger than females (0.25 m at birth; maximum 2.0 m).

Widespread in relatively moist environments, including marshlands. Diurnal; eats frogs, lizards and mice. Often encountered when flattened and sunbasking. If accidently stepped on or if otherwise provoked, this species will bite, but if given the opportunity will move away quietly.

Additional information on pp 13, 89, 93

Peter Robertson

Five-ringed Snake

Pseudonaja modesta

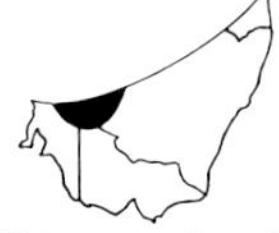

Small snake characterised by 4-7 (most often 5, rarely as many as 12) evenly spaced, narrow black bands across the body and tail. Background colouration is reddish brown or olive brown above and cream below with orange blotches. The bands may fade in older specimens and may be entirely absent, in which case it may be distinguished from other *Pseudonaja* species by having fewer ventral scales (less than 180 vs more than 180). May be further distinguished from banded juvenile Eastern Brown Snakes *P. textilis* by having less than 20 black bands across body. Average 0.4 m (0.18 m at hatching; maximum 0.6 m).

Found in arid sandy districts where it is active by day or night when not sheltering in lizard burrows. Preys mainly upon skinks. Disinclined to bite, but large specimens should be treated with respect.

Mark Hutchinson

Western Brown Snake
Pseudonaja nuchalis
dangerously venomous

Long and slender snake with narrow head. May be predominantly cream, tan or brown above, usually either with darker colouration over head and nape, or at least a few dark flecks or blotches over nape or neck. Some specimens have distinct dark cross-bands which are at least several scales wide. Differs from the Eastern Brown Snake *Pseudonaja textilis* and the King Brown Snake *Pseudechis australis* by the presence of a prominently enlarged and strap-like rostral (snout) scale. Differs from the Five-ringed Snake *P. modesta* by having more than 180 ventral scales. Average 1.2-1.5 m (0.25 m at hatching; maximum 1.8 m).

uvenile Specimen

.lex Dudley

This fast-moving species is widespread through arid districts. Will avoid trouble, but if provoked will bite. Eats rodents and lizards.

Additional information on pp 13, 89, 93

Greg Parker

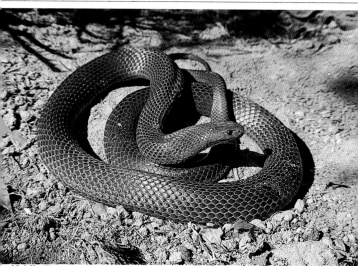

Mark Hutchinson

Eastern Brown Snake

Pseudonaja textilis (additional photos opposite)

dangerously venomous

Long and slender snake with narrow head. Adults usually uniform cream, tan, brown or grey above, sometimes with very faint, narrow cross bands, and occasionally with dark area over head. Belly usually cream or yellowish, usually with orange blotches, but in some older specimens, belly is grey. Juveniles (to 0.5 m) have a distinctive black region on top of the head, which is bordered by a pale reddish band across nape, followed behind by another black patch; the body may or may not have regularly spaced, narrow dark bands (if so, then these bands number more than 20). Differs from the King Brown Snake *Pseudechis australis* in having a narrower head and in the absence of the the lower temporal scale, which is always present in the King Brown Snake (see figure on page 39). The Eastern Brown Snake differs from the Western Brown Snake *Pseudonaja nuchalis* by having a much less pronounced rostral (snout) scale (in the Western Brown Snake this scale is quite prominently enlarged and strap-like). Also differs in having a pink (vs black) lining within mouth. Average 1.3 m (0.3 m at hatching; maximum 2.0 m).

This fast-moving species occurs mainly in sandy or dry country. It is amongst Australia's most dangerous snakes, being highly venomous, easily agitated, and often found in close proximity to human settlement. If cornered or surprised at close quarters, it will raise its body high in 'S' shaped loops, and may deliver several strikes in quick succession. Eats rodents and lizards. *Additional information on pp 13, 89, 93*

Robert Cook

juvenile 'unbanded' specimen juvenile 'banded' specimen

Greg Parker

Mark Hutchinson

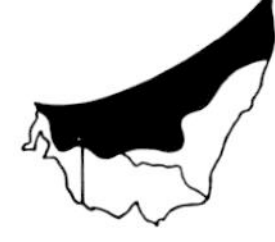

Coral Snake

Simoselaps australis

This species is readily identified by its distinctive reddish colour pattern and its unusual upturned snout - presumably modified to assist in burrowing. It is heavily built and has a proportionately short tail. Average 0.3 m (0.1 m at birth; maximum 0.4 m).

The coral snake is a nocturnal burrowing species sheltering by day in loose soil or beneath stumps, fallen timber or stones. It is known to eat small skinks as well as the eggs of lizards and snakes. Can occasionally be discovered moving about above ground and crossing roads late at night.

Additional information on page 12

Peter Robertso

Peter Robertson

Desert Banded Snake

Simoselaps bertholdii

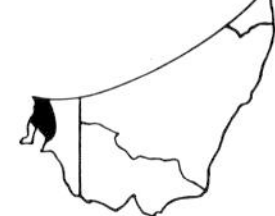

Yellowish-orange above with evenly spaced, broad black rings around body. The head is mainly white, finely peppered with black markings. It is heavily built, with a short tail. Average 0.25 m (0.1 m at hatching; maximum 0.35 m).

This is a 'sand-swimming' species which remains partially or totally submerged in sand at most times. It occasionally moves about on the surface - usually at night. It feeds primarily upon burrowing skinks.

Additional information on page 12

Mark Hutchinson

Greg Parker

Rough-scaled Snake
Tropidechis carinatus
dangerously venomous

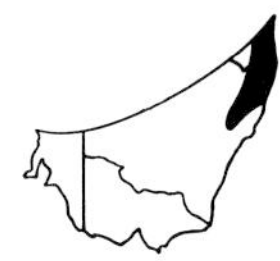

Olive-green to dark brown above, with narrow dark cross-bands. These cross-bands may be vague and generally become less apparent towards the tail. Each body scale has a faint to distinct ridge or keel transecting it from base to tip creating a rough texture to the skin. This dangerous species is frequently confused with the harmless Keelback Snake *Tropidonophis mairii*, which is sometimes found in the same habitats. Average 0.7 m (0.15-0.20 m at birth; maximum 1.0 m).

Usually found close to water in moist, forested country - often at high altitude. It is active more often at night than by day, especially in warm weather, when frogs, small mammals, and lizards are hunted. If molested it will bite savagely, sometimes resulting in life-threatening illness which may extend for weeks during hospitalization.

Additional information on pp 14, 89

Robert Cook

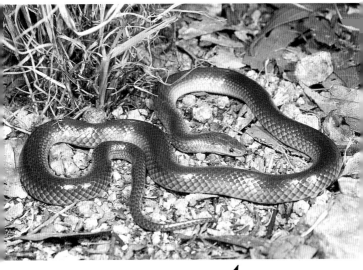

Carpentaria Snake

Unechis boschmai

Light to dark brown above. Scales may have dark edges resulting in a distinct pattern of reticulations. The presence of this dark colour may be concentrated above yielding a vague dark zone along the length of the back. Belly white. Head broad and flat, usually of lighter colour than body, and with very small eyes and pink tongue. Average 0.4 m (0.15 m at birth; maximum 0.5 m).

This is a nocturnal species, believed to feed mainly on skinks. The Carpentaria Snake is commonly found beneath logs, stones, railway sleepers and other debris. It is a nervous, jumpy snake that will not hesitate to bite if handled.

Gary Stephenson

Mark Hutchinson

Mark Hutchinso

Dwyer's Snake

Unechis dwyeri

Predominantly light to dark brown or reddish-brown above, each scale usually bearing a dark edge along its base. Rarely, an obscure dark line extends along the middle of the back (but only in specimens from outside the distribution range of the Southern Black-striped Snake *U. nigriceps*, with which it might otherwise be confused). Top of head and nape glossy black, bordered by cream or pale yellowish-brown along lips, tip of snout and area in front of eye. Belly cream. Differs from the Little Whip Snake *U. flagellum*, the Grey Snake *Hemiaspis damelii* and the Curl Snake *Denisonia suta* by having only 15 scale rows at mid-body. Average 0.3 m (0.18 m at birth; maximum 0.4 m).

Inhabits relatively dry forests and woodlands where it is most frequently found beneath stones or fallen timber. It is nocturnal and feeds mainly upon small skinks.

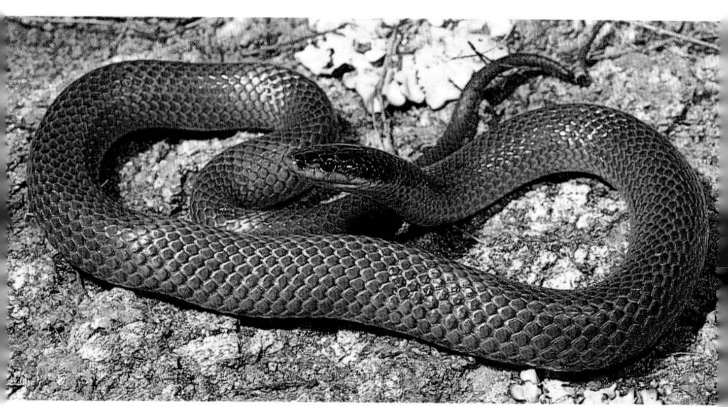

Mark Hutchinsc

Mark Hutchinson

Little Whip Snake
Unechis flagellum

Predominantly light to dark brown, greyish-brown or reddish-brown above; this colour is concentrated on the centre of each scale, while the base of each scale usually bears a dark edge, while a light margin extends along its exposed edge. Top of head and nape glossy black, bordered by pale brown or yellowish-brown along lips and tip of snout. This black region is usually interrupted by a pale bar that extends across snout between eye and nostril. In some high altitude populations the black region may be reduced to a small dark blotch. Belly colouration cream. The Little Whip Snake differs from all other *Unechis* species by having 17 rather than 15 scale rows at mid-body; and similarly, from the Curl Snake *Denisonia suta*, which has 19 mid-body scale rows. Average 0.3 m (0.18 m at birth; maximum 0.4 m).

This shy nocturnal species inhabits cool woodlands, dry forests and rocky areas where it is most frequently found beneath stones or fallen timber. Eats skinks.

Glenn Shea

Mark Hutchinson

Southern Black-striped Snake

Unechis nigriceps

Primarily dark greyish-brown to nearly black above, darkest along the top and centre of body, while this colour fades to a lighter shade of brown along flanks due to the presence of light brown margins along the exposed edges of scales. Belly white or cream. Distinguishable from other *Unechis* species within its geographic range by the presence of a dark vertebral stripe or zone. Average 0.4 m (0.2 m at birth; maximum 0.6 m).

This shy nocturnal species inhabits Mallee woodlands and other arid regions where it eats skinks and snakes.

Mark Hutchinson

Mark Hutchinson

Unechis spectabilis

Pale beige to red or reddish-brown above, this colour is concentrated on the centre of each scale, while each scale bears a dark base and a light margin along its exposed edge. Top of head and nape glossy black, bordered by pale patches both behind and in front of eye. The later usually extending upwards to form a bar across the snout. Belly and upper lip colouration white. This species differs from *U. nigriceps* by lacking vertebral stripe; from *U. flagellum* by having 15 rows of scales at midbody (vs 17); from *U. dwyeri* by its separate range of distribution; and from *Denisonia suta* by having only 15 (vs 19) rows of scales at midbody. Average 0.3 m (0.18 m at birth; maximum 0.5 m).

This shy nocturnal species inhabits arid, open woodlands and eats skinks.

ark Hutchinson

Glenn Shea

Bandy Bandy

Vermicella annulata

This extremely attractive snake differs from all other species in having broad black and white rings of similar breadth alternately encircling the body from snout to tail tip. Average 0.3-0.5 m (0.2 m at hatching; maximum 1.0 m).

The Bandy Bandy is a subterranean dwelling (and presumably burrowing) species that is only infrequently encountered – usually when it crosses roads at night or when uncovered beneath large stones or logs; in either case, especially after heavy rains. Feeds almost exclusively on Worm Snakes (genus *Ramphotyphlops*). Inoffensive by nature, it has a remarkable defensive display, flattening itself while arching one or two loops of its body high above the ground. This position may be held for some time. Not known to bite.

Peter Robertsc

A Green Tree Snake Dendrelaphis punctulatus *finds (above) and devours a frog (below and bottom right). This species is a common non-venomous inhabitant of the South-East, feeding primarily on frogs. Green Tree Snakes don't bother killing their prey prior to swallowing it, hence reports of freshly captured specimens disgorging live frogs! When upset or attacked, snakes often void their stomach contents, presumably to allow a faster escape.*

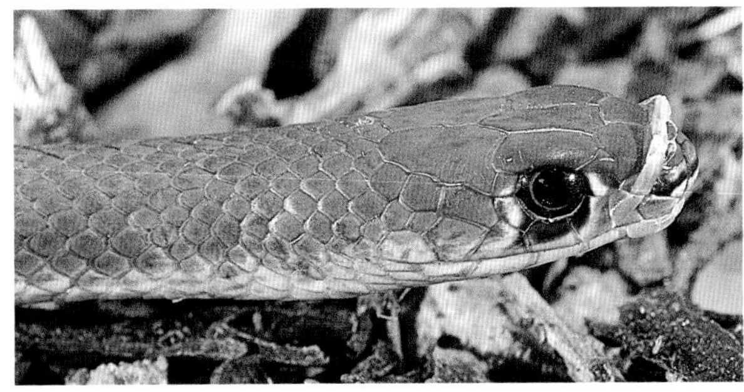

All snakes and lizards periodically slough the outer layer of their skin after producing a replacement layer underneath. During the interval between producing the new, and sloughing the old skin, the reptile takes on a dull, almost milky appearance as apparent in a Yellow-Faced Whip Snake (opposite page top). After a few days the milky hue disappears, indicating that the old skin is ready to be shed. In the case of snakes, the skin is usually peeled back, beginning at the snout (above), by rubbing against an object and simply crawling out of it. In this way the skin is removed in an inverted and often intact condition (middle of opposite page and below).

The reproduction of the Taipan Oxyuranus scutellatus. *Mating (top left, top right) occurs in spring or early summer. Egg laying (second from top) follows approximately two months later, followed by hatching after another two months (right, below). Note presence of tiny 'egg-tooth' used to slit egg-shell (right).*

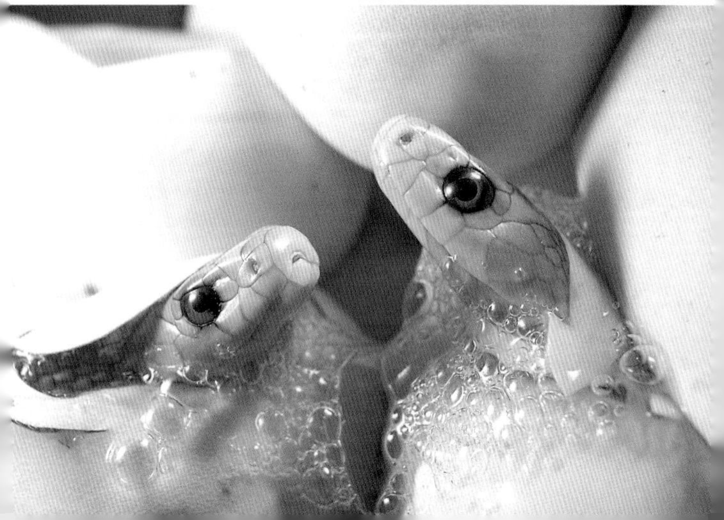

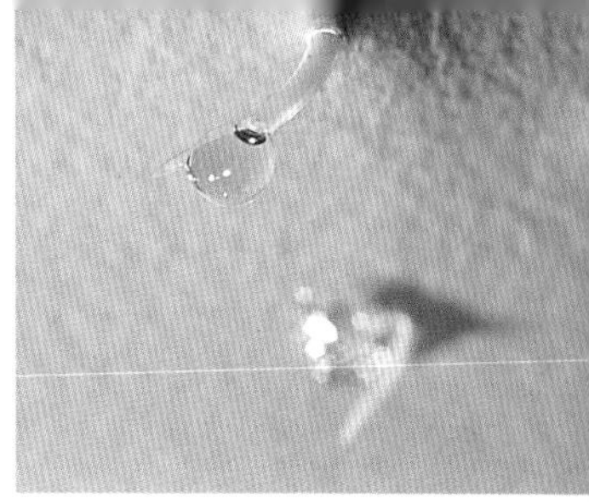

Unerring judgment and great dexterity are needed to obtain snake venoms from such dangerous species as the Tiger Snake. Long fangs penetrate a latex membrane stretched over a glass beaker. The beaker collects the venom which is freeze dried.

After drying, the venom crystals are carfully scraped from the beakers for weighing and packaging (below left). An inventory of dried venoms from a wide assortment of snake species is maintained at all times (below right).

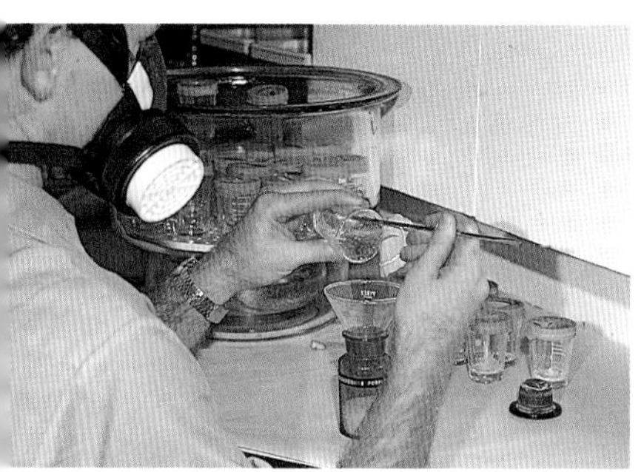

Australian snake venoms are amongst the most powerful animal toxins known. Dried venom from a single Tiger Snake milking (right, [top vial]), which would be far more than enough to cause a human fatality is compared with the accumulated venom from approximately 100 Tiger Snake milkings (left), 300 Brown Snake milkings (centre), and 100 Black Snake milkings (right).

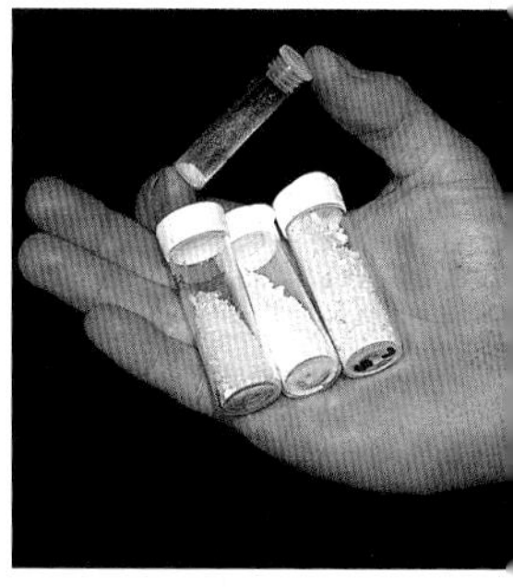

With the life-saving importance of the venom production work at the Australian Reptile Park, over 200 venomous snakes must be maintained, all in separate cages (above left). Numerous species are bred and reared in the facility to reduce the need for collection from the wild. The young are reared in small plastic nursery cages (above right).

Facilities at the Australian Reptile Park are made available for the use of biologists and researchers on an 'on call' basis. Work done with the reptiles in recent years has contributed to the pool of scientific knowledge.

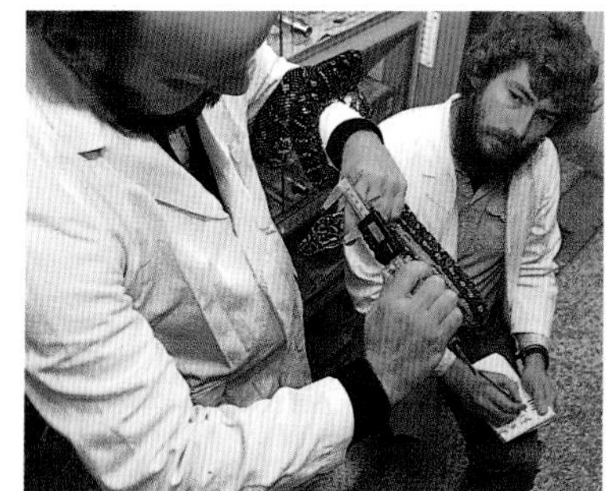

During the twice daily reptile demonstrations (below left) visitors get a close look at various reptiles and are provided with the opportunity to see a deadly snake milked, a demonstration of the pressure/immobilization technique for treating snake-bite and a supervised opportunity to touch a harmless snake. The Reptile Park education centre is a fun place for school groups to learn about Australian wildlife (below right).

Dangerous Snakes

SNAKE VENOMS AND ANTIVENOMS

The South-East has the distinction of providing a home for some of the most dangerously venomous snakes in the world. Although the bites of many of the venomous species are no more severe than wasp or bull-ant stings, eleven species which occur in the region are regarded as dangerously venomous. These are the Taipan, Common and Black Tiger Snakes, Death Adder, Red-bellied and Spotted Black Snakes, King Brown Snake, Eastern and Western Brown Snakes, Rough-scaled Snake and Copperhead. The venoms of these species may be far more potent than necessary for the snake to overcome and kill its prey. The Taipan, for instance, carries enough venom to kill 12,000 guinea pigs in a single bite. The extreme toxicity of the Taipan's venom allows it to make 'snap-bites' whereby the prey is released, but unable to move far away before succombing to the powerful toxins.

Snake venom is a highly developed form of saliva, injected by the snake into its victim through hollow, modified fangs. Fangs are easily blunted or wrenched out in the struggles of prey animals, but fresh fangs are always held in reserve; each poised to move into position when required. The base of a functioning fang, and often the first reserve fang behind it as well, is penetrated by a duct that leads from a large gland behind the eye. These glands, one on either side of the head, are modified salivary glands surrounded by muscle. When these muscles contract, they force the clear or yellowish venom along the venom ducts and down through the fangs, squirting it out under pressure as if from a pair of hypodermic syringes. Snakes do not normally inject all of their venom reserves in a single bite - enough is left for each of a possible series of consecutive bites. Interestingly however, venom is not always injected.

The venom of each species of snake is unique, consisting of a combination of complex proteins which act on the prey or bite victim in various ways. In most dangerous Australian species, the major action of the venom is its effect upon the victim's nervous system, hindering the operation of muscles and causing paralysis which can lead to death from paralysis of the diaphram and asphyxiation, or heart failure. Other components present in the venoms of certain species act to destroy blood cells, to cause blood clots or excessive bleeding, or to destroy tissue. Typical early symptoms of bites where significant envenomation has occurred include severe headache, nausea, vomiting, confusion, temporary loss of consciousness, rapid pulse and tender lymph nodes. Later signs of envenomation may include drooping eyelids, voice change, double vision, difficulty in swallowing and intense abdominal pain which can be followed by the vomiting of blood.

Antivenoms are produced by the Commonwealth Serum Laboratories in Melbourne. Snake venom is forwarded from the Australian Reptile Park to the laboratories where, after being processed, it is injected into Percheron horses. Over 250 horses take part in the antivenom program, all living a life of luxury. They undergo minimal stress during the inoculation and extraction processes. Inoculation is quite harmless, and extraction is as simple as donating blood is for humans.

The horses are given increasing doses of venom over a period of time until they have built up sufficient antibodies to the venom. When this occurs, antibodies are extracted from the blood, purified and reduced to a useable form.

The antivenoms taken from the horses are used to treat humans suffering from snake envenomation. Injected into the human bloodstream, the antibodies attack the venom, neutralising its effects. The dose and type of antivenom given to a patient vary according to the species responsible for the bite and, when it can be ascertained, the amount of venom injected. The age and weight of the victim makes no difference to the dose of antivenom required in the treatment.

FIRST AID FOR SNAKE-BITE

First aid treatment of snake-bite was revolutionized in the early 1980s by the work of Dr Struan Sutherland and his research team at the Commonwealth Serum Laboratories. It was shown that the movement of the venom into the bloodstream can be retarded for many hours if firm pressure is applied over the bitten area and the limb is immobilized. The following first aid treatment for bites to the limbs from venomous snakes and funnel-web spiders is recommended in the publication – First Aid for Snake Bite in Australia by Dr Sutherland, published by the Commonwealth Serum Laboratories.

"Apply a broad pressure bandage over the bite site as soon as possible. If no bandages are available, use stockings, strips of clothing, etc. The bandage should be as tight as you would apply to a sprained ankle or wrist. Extend the bandages as high as possible (preferably to arm-pit or groin). Next, apply a splint (a suitably sized and shaped branch will do) to the affected leg or arm. Bind it firmly to as much of the limb as possible."

If the bandages and splint have been applied correctly, they will be comfortable and may be left on for several hours. They must not be taken off until the patient has reached medical care. The doctor will decide when to remove the bandages. If venom has been injected it will move into the blood stream and produce effects very quickly when the bandages are removed.

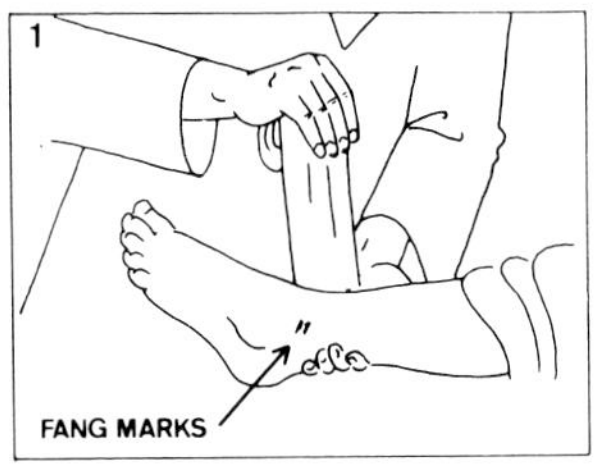

1. Apply a broad pressure bandage over the bite site as soon as possible (don't take off jeans as the movement of doing so will assist venom to enter the blood stream. Keep the bitten leg still!).

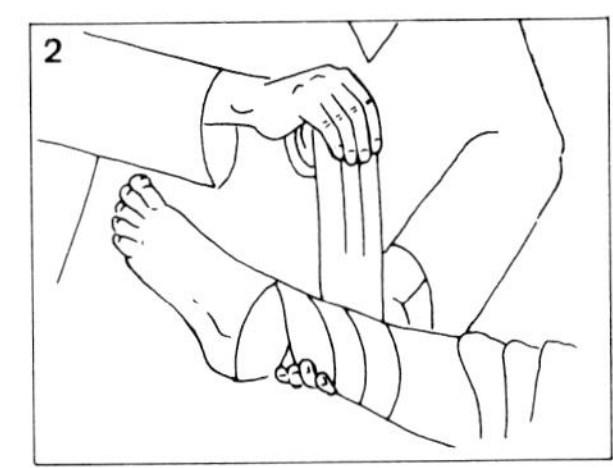

2. The bandage should be as tight as you would apply to a sprained ankle.

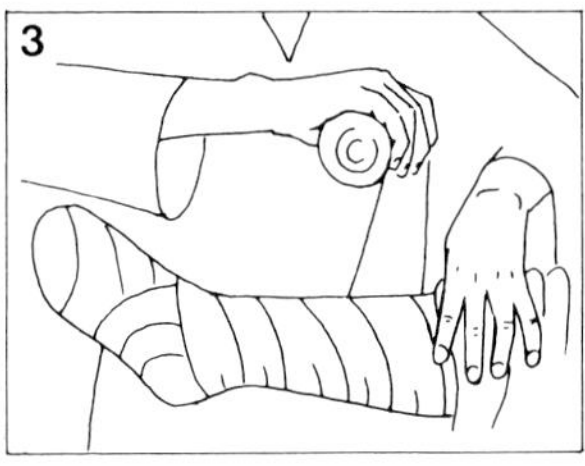

3. Extend the bandages as high as possible.

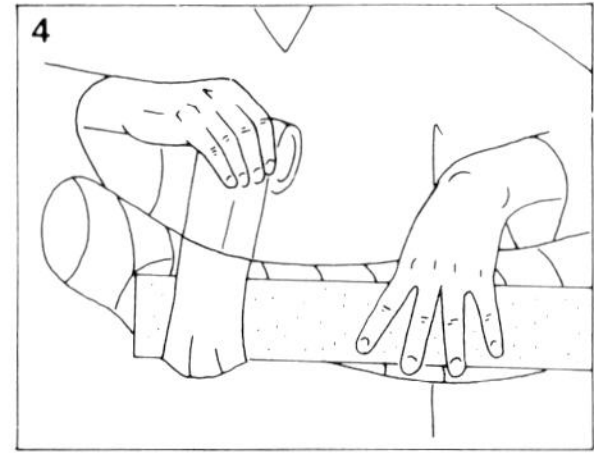

4. Apply a splint to the leg.

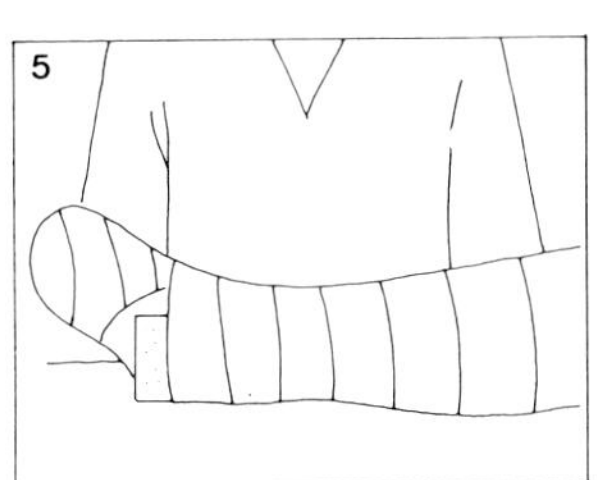

5. Bind it firmly to as much of the leg as possible.

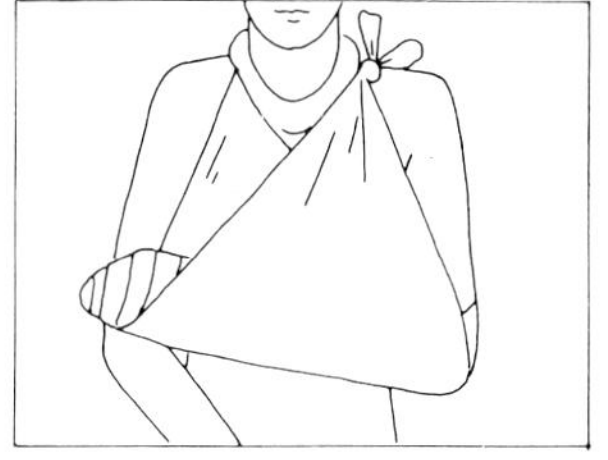

Bites on hand or forearm. **1.** Bind to elbow with bandages. **2.** Use splint to elbow. **3.** Use sling.

Figure 14. Diagramatic representation of first aid treatment for snake-bite victims (after Dr. Struan Sutherland of the Commonwealth Serum Laboratories, [1979], *Family Guide to Dangerous Animals and Plants of Australia*).

It is not possible to decide whether or not a snake is venomous by the shape of its head or the formation of the puncture marks on a victim. Only rarely does a dangerous snake neatly embed its two front fangs and leave two distinct punctures. Typically a series of scratches are left - the same type of wounds may be left by teeth of an innocuous species. Therefore, in the event of a bite from any snake that cannot be identified with 100% confidence, the pressure immobilization first aid treatment described above should be applied and medical advice sought.

There are a few "don'ts" to consider following a snake-bite incident. *Don't* try to catch or kill the snake responsible for the bite - it wastes time and can lead to additional, possibly more serious bites. *Don't* wash the wound; residual venom can be used by the doctor to identify the snake species. *Don't* attempt to cut into the wound as this will spread the venom into the bloodstream and can damage nerves, blood vessels and tendons. *Don't* panic; it is extremely unlikely that the bite will be life-threatening. Of the 3,000 or so reported snake bites in Australia each year, only 300 yield significant signs of envenomation leading to antivenom being used. Of these, there are only, on average, between one and six human deaths per year due to snake-bite in a population of over 16 million people.

AVOIDING SNAKE-BITE

Snakes are shy, secretive creatures that avoid confrontations with humans and other larger animals whenever possible. After all, snakes have nothing to gain from such encounters and everything to lose. Even the largest and most venomous snakes typically flee from approaching bushwalkers, gliding away into burrows, hollow logs or rock crevices without being seen. Others will lay still and rely upon natural camouflage to remain unnoticed. Often an entire group of bushwalkers can pass by a snake, only to have one of the last members of the procession point out the snake to those who nearly stepped on it.

There are some simple guidelines to follow that can reduce the chance of snake-bite accidents occurring. Familiarization with the identification and habits of the dangerous snake species that inhabit a given area can help, and this book will hopefully assist in this. Protective clothing is recommended; long trousers and boots reduce the chances of being bitten. Always carry a crepe bandage for use in the first aid treatment of snake-bite and know how to use it (see pp 90-91 of this book).

Large venomous snakes are attracted to areas with sufficient cover and a healthy population of rats and mice - conditions often created when building materials and other debris are left in piles around rural homes and properties, particularly in agricultural areas or where food is otherwise available to rodent pests.

Relying on solar energy to raise their body temperature, snakes enter a period of relative inactivity during the colder winter months in the south-east and are less likely to be seen. During the warm spring and summer months (the breeding season for many species) most snakes become especially active and bushwalkers should keep a watch on the trail in front of them. This is especially true when walking in the vicinity of tall grass tussocks or near freshwater rivers or creeks - areas where snakes often abound.

Copperheads and Tiger Snakes can be gregarious and live in relatively concentrated numbers, especially near swamps and waterways where an abundance of their favorite food, frogs, occur. Red-bellied Black Snakes also prey heavily upon frogs and may be found in relatively high concentrations near water.

While most snakes will give way to the bushwalker before being sighted themselves, snakes can be extremely lethargic while 'sunbaking' and may be accidentally stepped upon. Some species have a peak period of activity immediately following sunset. Nocturnal snakes such as King Brown Snakes and Death Adders do not always flee at the approach of danger, but may 'freeze', relying upon the darkness and camouflage. Protective footwear is especially important for hikers at dusk or night.

Snakes rarely if ever actually chase people, but if cornered or confronted in open areas where escape would be unlikely, some may adopt a threatening posture from which to lash out. Brown snakes and Taipans raise their heads above 'S' shaped body loops, displaying yellow belly scales as a warning. This may be accompanied by a slow and deliberate flickering of the tongue, threatening hisses, and short lunges in the direction of the perceived danger. Other species flatten themselves horizontally, and may strike sideways towards their enemies. When flattened, Death Adders and some Tiger Snakes display vivid colours normally hidden between the scales.

If a snake has nowhere else to go, it may try to get past you; there are many stories of snakes crossing over or between feet and moving away as quickly as possible. Unfortunately, some people will attempt to kill or catch the snakes they encounter, leading to a large proportion of serious bites from snakes each year. Purposely killing any snake, apart from being potentially very dangerous, is rarely justifiable and is illegal in most States. Snakes are an important part of the Australian environment and as such should be preserved. Snakes encountered on residential properties can often be moved by representatives of the wildlife protection authority in your region (see Table 1, page 98 for a list of statutory wildlife authorities in the South-East); otherwise they should be able to suggest a nearby museum, zoological park, pest control company, animal care and rehabilitation group, or private herpetologist who can move the snake to a more isolated area.

Observing Snakes

It is anticipated that many of the readers of this book will be avid naturalists who will go out of their way to find and identify as many different species of snakes as possible. More and more Australians are beginning to lay aside hysterical disdain for the snakes to recognize that the snakes are a fascinating group of animals worthy of further study.

The time of year and the time of day are very important when planning an outing to observe snakes in the wild. Many species are active primarily at night or only during evening and morning hours. Others are active during daylight hours. These may bask in the sun but are quick to get out of sight at the slightest commotion. Throughout much of the South-East snakes become dormant in winter, though in the warmer, northerly part of this region it is warm enough for them to remain active throughout the year. Cool weather slows all reptiles however, and they do not become active again until the weather warms.

In most areas, snakes are considerably more common than most people believe. Snakes are generally wary and secretive, and observing them requires patience, but if you know their activities and habitats, you'll quickly become proficient at spotting these elusive animals and locating their retreats. Snakes are found in nearly every type of habitat in the South-East: along the sides of streams, ponds, lakes, wooded hillsides, sandhill country, desert country, rainforests, etc. Look under flat rocks, pieces of bark or logs - favorite retreats of snakes. Piles of construction debris as well as abandoned farm buildings and their attendant rubble are ideal snake haunts. Snakes may appear on rural roads when temperatures exceed 25° C. The best roads are heat-retaining sealed roads that pass through relatively undisturbed habitats. A four-hour peroid beginning about an hour before dusk - just after an afternoon shower is the ideal time.

If you do not have the time, patience or endurance to observe snakes in the wild, an alternative is to visit your local zoological park (Table 2 on page 98 lists zoological parks in the South-East exhibiting large collections of snakes). If planning a trip through the Sydney region, spend a day at the Australian Reptile Park in Gosford. The famous facility has one of the most varied collections of native reptiles in Australia and a reputation for being the most entertaining and educational zoological facility of its kind. There you will be able to see all of the dangerously venomous species of the South-East, some behind glass, others in pits, and have the opportunity to hold friendly non-venomous varieties during the twice daily reptile demonstrations.

Maintaining Snakes in Captivity

The maintenance of some species of snakes can be a fascinating and educational experience for the whole family, with a number of advantages over the keeping of more conventional pets. Relatively little space is required; accommodation (such as a well-decorated terrarium) can be aesthetically pleasing, and the reptiles themselves are clean, quiet and non-demanding, given a few simple requirements. However, before any attempt is made to collect or otherwise obtain snakes for captive maintenance and observations, it must be understood that they are all protected by law. These laws generally carry with them substantial fines and penalties for non-compliance. The laws regulating the keeping of reptiles in captivity vary considerably from State to State and can be determined by contacting the relevant authority in your State or Territory. These are listed in Table 1 on page 98.

Never collect snakes just for the sake of collecting them. Keeping a snake on impulse will almost certainly be at the expense of the animal's well being. It has been the custom for some herpetological hobbyists (and professionals) to express their interests by "going collecting" - merely trying to find and bag as many species or specimens (or both) as possible. Even though the specimens may be returned to their home territories later, the lives of many snakes are unduly disrupted, often fatally, and seldom is as much learned about them as could be discovered by simply observing the animals without unduly disturbing them. You should be well prepared for the housing of any snakes before they arrive.

Never contemplate collecting snakes without a thorough knowledge of what dangerous species occur in the area. It is not recomended that dangerously (or potentially dangerously) venomous species be collected or otherwise handled.

Snakes must be collected in a sensible manner that leaves the habitat as nearly as possible exactly as you found it. There is no reasonable excuse for chopping down trees, using a pinch-bar to loosen and possibly damage rock exfoliations, or otherwise inflicting damage to the area you choose to carry out your search. Under no circumstances should snakes be collected in national parks or other wildlife reserves. If your search is to be carried out on private property you must first obtain the permission of the property owner.

It is a good idea for hobbyists to join a herpetological society or naturalists club (see Table 3, page 99 for a listing of herpetological associations in the South-East). The contact with similarly interested and often highly experienced people can provide a valuable source of information on the subject of care and breeding of reptiles. I would also recommend that anyone contemplating the captive maintenance of reptiles should purchase or borrow a copy of *Care of Australian Reptiles in*

Captivity (144pp; John Weigel, 1988, published by the Reptile Keepers Association). This is the only publication currently available that adequately provides the novice with the basic information required for keeping Australian reptiles in a healthy and well adjusted state.

Conservation

The conservation needs of snakes in the South-East are similar to those of other forms of wildlife in the area. But for the fact that rugged country throughout much of the Great Dividing Range is useless for agricultural or commercial use, there would have been little left of the natural environnment of the South-East. Land clearing, overgrazing and the introduction of feral pests have seen the substantial degradation of most of the region. Although there has been a general reduction in areas where snakes occur, no Australian snake species is yet known to have become extinct since white settlement. Agricultural activities may have actually aided a few rodent-eating species, such as the Eastern Brown Snake by producing a greater supply of food. Apart from the effects of agriculture and habitat clearing, the predatory activities of feral cats and foxes must severly affect some snake species (and their prey). The collection of snakes for museum study or captive care and observation has never been shown to have any impact on populations, nor has the killing of snakes that is still an unfortunate (and dangerous) tradition in Australia.

Selected References for Further Reading

Banks, C. (1980) *Keeping Reptiles and Amphibians as Pets*, Nelson, Melbourne, 129pp.

Cogger, H. G. (1980) *Snakes*, Science Field Guide Series: Longman Cheshire, Sydney, 38pp.

Cogger, H. G. (1986) *Reptiles and Amphibians of Australia*, Reed Books, Sydney, 688pp, 4th revised edition.

Covacevich, J. (1968) The Snakes of Brisbane, Queensland Museum, Brisbane.

Grigg, G., R. Shine and H. Ehmann (eds.) (1985) *Biology of Australian Frogs and Reptiles*, Surrey Beatty & Sons, Sydney, 527pp.

Jenkins, R. and R. Bartell (1980) *A Field Guide to the Reptiles of the Australian High Country*, Inkata Press, Melbourne, 278pp.

Mirtschin, P. and R. Davis (1982) *Dangerous Snakes of Australia. An Illustrated Guide to Australia's Most Venomous Snakes*, Rigby, Adelaide, 207pp.

Parker, H. W. and A. G. C. Grandison (1977) *Snakes: a Natural History*, University of Queensland Press, St Lucia, 124pp, 2nd edition.

Schmida, Gunther (1985) *The Cold-Blooded Australians*, Doubleday, Sydney, 208pp.

Sutherland, S. (1981) *Venomous Creatures of Australia*, Oxford University Press, Melbourne, 128pp.

Sutherland, S. (1983) *Australian Animal Toxins, The Creatures, Their Toxins, and Care of the Poisoned Patient*, Oxford University Press, Melbourne, 527pp.

Swann, G. (1990) *Field Guide to the Snakes and Lizards of New South Wales*, Three Sisters Productions, Sydney, (in press).

Weigel, J. (1988) *Care of Australian Reptiles in Captivity*, Reptile Keepers Association, Gosford, 144pp.

Wilson, S. and D. Knowles (1988) *Australian Lizards and Snakes: a Photographic Reference to the Terrestrial Reptiles of Australia*, Collins, Sydney, 448pp.

Worrell, E. (1963) *Reptiles of Australia*, Angus and Robertson, Sydney, 208pp.

Table 1. Statutory wildlife authorities in the South-East.

Australian Capital Territory	
ACT Parks and Conservation Service,	
PO Box 158, Canberra City, 2601.	Tel. (062) 46 2849.
New South Wales	
NSW National Parks and Wildlife Service,	
Box 1967, Hurstville, 2250.	Tel. (02) 585 6444.
Queensland	
National Parks and Wildlife Service,	
138 Albert Street, Brisbane, 4000.	Tel. (07) 227 5547.
Victoria	
National Parks and Wildlife Division,	
123 Brown Street, Heidelberg, 3084.	Tel. (03) 450 8600.
South Australia	
National Parks and Wildlife Service,	
GPO Box 1782, Adelaide, 5001.	Tel. (08) 216 7777.
Tasmania	
Department of Land, Parks and Wildlife,	
PO Box 44A, Hobart, 7005.	Tel. (002) 30 2610.

Table 2. Zoological parks in the South-East with large collections of snakes.

Adelaide Zoological Gardens, Adelaide, SA	(08) 267 3255
Australian Reptile Park, Gosford Nth, NSW	(043) 28 4311
Ballarat Reptile & Wildlife Park, Ballarat East, Vic	(053) 32 3229
Bredl's Reptile Park, Renmark, SA	(085) 85 1431
Healesville Sanctuary, Healesville, Vic	(059) 62 4022
Melbourne Zoological Gardens, Melbourne, Vic	(03) 347 1522
Queensland Reptile and Fauna Park, Beerwah, Qld	(071) 94 1134
Taronga Park Zoo, Mosman, NSW	(02) 969 2777

Table 3. Amateur herpetological societies in the South-East.

Australian Herpetological Society
PO Box R-79, Royal Exchange,
Sydney, NSW, 2000

ACT Herpetological Group
c/- ACT Parks and Conservation,
PO Box 158 Canberra City, 2601

Reptile Keepers Association
PO Box 98,
Gosford, NSW, 2250

Reptile Keepers Associaton of South-East Queensland
c/- 9 Grey Street,
Ipswich, Qld, 4305

Reptile Keepers Association of South Australian
c/- 12 Julia Crescent
Woodcroft (Adelaide), SA, 5162

South Australian Herpetology Group
c/- South Australian Museum,
N. Terrace, Adelaide, SA, 5000

Victorian Herpetology Group
PO Box 60,
Coldstream, Vic, 3770

Victorian Herpetological Society
c/- 16 Suspension Street,
Ardeer, Vic, 3022

Table 4. Summary of relevant scale conditions for pythons, colubrids and elapids. For the most part, the figures are derived from H. G. Cogger (1986) *Reptiles and Amphibians of Australia*. Reed, Sydney.

	mid-bodies	ventrals	anal	subcaudals
BOIDAE				
Liasis maculosus	35-45	240-295	single	30-35, divided
Morelia spilota	40-51	240-310	usually single	60-95, divided
COLUBRIDAE				
Boiga irregularis	19-23	225-265	single	80-130, divided
Dendrelaphis punctulatus	13-15	180-230	divided	100-150, divided
Tropidonophis mairii	15 -17	130-165	divided	50-85, divided
ELAPIDAE				
Acanthophis antarcticus	21-23	110-130	single	35-60, mostly single
Austrelaps superbus	13-17	140-165	single	35-65, mostly single
Cacophis harrietae	15	170-200	divided	25,45, divided
C. krefftii	15	140-160	divided	25-40. divided
C. squamulosus	15	165-185	divided	30-50, divided
Cryptophis nigrescens	15	165-210	single	30-45, single
Demansia atra	15	160-220	divided	70-95, divided
Demansia psammophis	15	165-230	divided	60-105, divided
Denisonia devisii	17	120-150	single	20-40, single
D. suta	19-21	140-190	single	20-35, single
Drysdalia coronoides	15	130-160	single	35-70, single
D. mastersii	15	130-160	single	40-55, single
D. rhodogaster	15	141-155	single	40-55, single
Echiopsis curta	19	130-145	single	30-39, single
Furina diadema	15	160-210	divided	35-70, divided
Hemiaspis damelii	17	140-170	divided	35-50, single
H. signata	17	150-170	divided	40-60, single
Hoplocephalus bitorquatus	19-21	190-225	single	40-65, single
H. bungaroides	21	200-230	single	40-65, single
H. stephensii	21	220-250	single	50-70, single
Notechis ater	17	163-173	single	40-60, single
N. scutatus	17-19	140-190	single	35-65, single
Oxyuranus scutellatus	21-23	220-250	single	45-80, divided
Pseudechis australis	17	189-220	divided	50-75, first few from vent single, remainder divided
P. guttatus	19	175-205	divided	45-65, as for *P. australis*
P. porphyriacus	17	180-210	divided	40-65, as for *P. australis*, or all single
Pseudonaja modesta	17	145-175	divided	35-55, divided
P. nuchalis	17-19	180-230	divided	50-70, divided
P. textilis	17	185-235	divided	45-75, divided, or first few from vent single

Simoselaps australis	17	140-170	usually divided	15-30, divided
S. bertholdii	17	140-175	divided	15-30, divided
Unechis boschmai	15	145-190	single	20-35, single
U. dwyeri	15	147-152	single	20-40, single
U. flagellum	17	125-150	single	20-40, single
U. nigriceps	15	140-175	single	15-35, single
U. spectabilis	15	135-168	single	20-40, single
Tropidechis carinatus	23	160-185	single	50-60, single
Vermicella annulata	15	180-320	divided	12-30, divided

Table 5. Summary of relevant scale conditions of worm snakes (family Typhlopidae). For the most part, the figures are derived from H. G. Cogger (1986) *Reptiles and Amphibians of Australia*. Reed, Sydney.

	midbodies	**nasal cleft**	**bodylength/ diameter**
Ramphotyphlops affinis	18	contacts second supralabial	45-60
R. australis	22	contacts second supralabial	25-50
R. bituberculatus	20	contacts second supralabial	40-90
R. ligatus	24	contacts first supralabial	20-40
R. nigrescens	22	contacts first supralabial	30-60
R. proximus	20	contacts first supralabial	20-40
R. wiedii	20	contacts second supralabial	30-80

Index